MACHINERY AND LABOR

LONDON : HUMPHREY MILFORD
OXFORD UNIVERSITY PRESS

CHAPTERS ON
MACHINERY AND LABOR

BY

GEORGE E. BARNETT
PROFESSOR OF STATISTICS IN THE JOHNS HOPKINS UNIVERSITY

CAMBRIDGE
HARVARD UNIVERSITY PRESS
1926

PRINTED AT THE HARVARD UNIVERSITY PRESS
CAMBRIDGE, MASS., U. S. A.

PREFACE

The present essay seeks to contribute to the better understanding of a problem which has engaged the interest and sympathy of many writers — the displacement of skill by machinery. There are few persons who do not recognize in the introduction of machinery an important means of increasing the national income, and of improving the condition of labor as a whole. But this advance in well-being is frequently bought at the price of hardship to the workers in the trades directly affected.

This study is based upon an intensive examination of concrete cases of the introduction of machinery. The first four chapters set forth the facts relating to the introduction of four machines: the linotype, the stone-planer, the semi-automatic bottle machine, and the automatic bottle machine. Each of these chapters contains an estimate of the potential and actual displacement from the trade, a description of the policy of the trade union concerned, and a summary of the effects on the wages and other conditions of employment of the hand-workers left in employment. In the last two chapters, the facts thus presented are brought into relation with the current theories (1) as to the mechanical and economic factors governing the amount of displacement, and (2) as to the proper policy for a trade union to pursue when the skill of its members is threatened with displacement.

Chapter I was originally published in the *Yale Review*, November, 1904, chapter II, in the *Journal of Political Economy*, May, 1916, chapters III–VI, in the *Quarterly Journal of Economics*, May, August, November, 1925 and February, 1926. A few unimportant changes have been made. I am indebted to the publishers of these journals for permission to use this material in the present connection.

G. E. B.

CONTENTS

MACHINERY AND LABOR

CHAPTER I

THE INTRODUCTION OF THE LINOTYPE

SUMMARY

In 1887, typesetting was essentially the same art as in the sixteenth century. While other branches of the printing trade had been revolutionized, the compositor had not advanced in his processes beyond the point he had reached four hundred years before. Probably no other handicraft employing such a large number of persons underwent as little change during this period, so full of industrial reconstruction. Since 1890, machine composition has been rapidly supplanting typesetting by hand. The machine is still constantly encroaching on the field of the hand compositor, but the period of introduction may be properly considered as concluded with the year 1903. By that time, the craft had adjusted itself to the new conditions and the future trend of events could be foreseen with some clearness.

It is the purpose of the present chapter to estimate the displacement of labor due to the linotype,[1] to describe the policy pursued by the union printers with

1. There are several kinds of typesetting and typecasting machines, but the Mergenthaler linotype exercised such a predominant influence that attention may be confined to it without danger of serious error. According to the returns made by local unions to the Secretary of the International Typographical Union, the total number of typesetting and typecasting machines of all makes in operation, on January 1, 1904, in union and non-union offices within the jurisdiction of six hundred and twenty-five local unions, was 7,129, and of these 6,375 were linotypes. The proportion of linotypes was probably not quite so great outside the territory covered by the Typographical Union, but the correction required would not be very great.

reference to the machine and the economic effects of the machine on the workmen engaged in the trade, and finally to examine how far the policy of the International Typographical Union may be successfully adopted by other trade-unions during periods of machine introduction.

I

The displacement of hand compositors by the introduction of the linotype may be estimated with some accuracy and will afford an index to the industrial disturbance involved. The following table gives the number of linotypes manufactured in the United States and Canada for each year from 1887 to 1903:

1887	55	1896	757
1888	66	1897	510
1889	57	1898	636
1890	57	1899	566
1891	69	1900	714
1892	288	1901	661
1893	568	1902	757
1894	890	1903	891
1895	1,076		
		Total	8,618

Of the 8,618 machines manufactured, somewhat less than five hundred were shipped out of the United States and Canada and an approximately equal number were destroyed by fire or otherwise put out of use. About 7,500 linotypes were in operation in the United States and Canada on January 1, 1904.[2]

The average rate of composition on the linotype is estimated by competent authorities at between 4,000 and 5,000 ems per hour. The rate of hand composition does not exceed 1,000 ems per hour on the average. A linotype operator is therefore able to set as much in one

2. The officials of the Mergenthaler Linotype Company kindly supplied data on which the above estimate was based.

hour as a hand compositor does in four. Assuming that the 7,500 machines were in operation the same number of hours each day as hand compositors formerly worked, the potential displacement of hand compositors to January 1, 1904, may be reckoned at 30,000. Two modifications must, however, be made in this calculation. In the first place, many linotypes were worked by two or three shifts of operators.[3] The number of machine operators in the United States, operating 7,129 machines of all makes, within the jurisdiction of the International Typographical Union on January 1, 1904, was 10,604, or approximately 150 per cent of the number of machines.[4] If allowance is made for this fact, the estimate of potential displacement is increased to 45,000 hand compositors. Some deduction must be made from this total on account of the reduction in working hours. The hand compositor worked on the average about ten hours per day, while linotype operators in 1904 did not average more than eight hours.[5] Deducting 20 per cent for this cause, we may finally estimate the potential displacement of hand compositors at 36,000.

The actual displacement was far less than the potential displacement. A large part of the 7,500 linotypes would never have come into use if the economies incident to their operation had not been so large as to lead to an increase in the amount of printing done. An examination of the table on the preceding page points to the conclusion that the years 1894, 1895 and 1896 were marked by a large amount of actual displacement of hand compositors.[6] The rapid introduction of machines

3. See The Typographical Journal, February, 1904, p. 212.
4. Idem.
5. See page 20 for the data on which this calculation is made.
6. Additional evidence to this effect is found in the many complaints of displacement contained during these years in The Typographical Journal, the official journal of the union printers. These decrease greatly after 1896.

in these years resulted chiefly from the desire of newspaper publishers to reduce the cost of composition. A considerable part of the more moderate increase of machines since 1896 has been due to an increasing demand for printed matter.

Even, however, during the earlier period, there is evidence that the actual displacement was not nearly so great as the estimate of potential displacement would indicate. The following statistics compiled from a report made in 1895 by Mr. Wm. Ferguson, Secretary of the New York Typographical Union to the New York Labor Commissioner, throw considerable light on this point.[7]

Number of offices included in investigation	15
Number of linotypes in use	293
Average number of ems set on a linotype in an hour	3,445
Number of printers employed before the introduction of machines	1,512
Number of substitutes employed before the introduction of machines	396
Number of printers employed after the introduction of machines	968
Percentage of decrease	36

The figures given include the whole working force of printers, many of whom on account of the character of their work were entirely unaffected by the machine. It appears that 293 linotypes displaced 544 printers. The actual displacement in these offices in the initial stage of the introduction of the machine was therefore at the rate of less than two printers for each machine.

This difference between the potential displacement of hand compositors and the actual displacement of printers in the early period was due to several causes. First and most important was the practice of putting men already at work as hand compositors in charge of ma-

7. Annual Report of the Commissioner of Labor of the State of New York, 1895, vol. i, pp. 370–372.

chines. The 293 machines were manned by from 300 to 400 journeymen printers. The displacement of hand compositors was therefore much greater than the displacement of printers. Also, the speed of the machine operators was less than it was later. The average number of ems set per hour, it will be noted, was found to be 3,445. The rate of 4,000 to 5,000 ems was attained only after a considerable part of the operators had been some years at the machine.

Altho the great increase in the demand for the machine product naturally came after the machine had been somewhat generally introduced, even in the introductory period the cheapness of machine composition led to an increase in the amount of composition done. For some years prior to the introduction of the linotype, the practice of using "plate matter" had been growing among newspaper publishers, the high cost of hand composition having forced the publishers to the use of an undesirable substitute. The extension of this practice had been for many years a frequent occasion of friction between the publishers and the local unions of the International Typographical Union. The low cost of linotype composition caused in most machine offices an entire abandonment of the use of "plate matter," resulting in an immediate increase of printers' work. Also, the producing power of the composing room was increased in order to secure a greater effectiveness during the last few hours before going to press. Editors cancelled machine-set matter with much less reluctance. To a casual observer, the composition of a newspaper would appear an unpromising field for the operation of the law of elasticity of demand, but the common experience of printers and publishers indicates that in numerous ways the cheapening of the cost of composition acted as an immediate stimulant to the demand.

In the second period, roughly designated as beginning with the year 1897, consumers shared more largely in the economy of production resulting from the use of the linotype. The larger profits of newspaper publishers led to strong competition which partly took the form of an increase in the size of the newspapers. The linotypes installed for this purpose did not displace hand compositors, but on the contrary enlarged the field of employment for those printers who could learn the operation of the machine.[8] In the book and job trade, the cheapening of the product through competition caused an enormous increase in the amount of composition done. As early as 1896, the *American Bookmaker*, a trade journal, naïvely complained that "employing printers foolishly give to the public advantages which should accrue to them. . . . It is probably safe to suggest that not one in ten of those who have adopted typesetting machines are making any more net profit than they did when all of their type was set by hand."[9] The result was that after 1897 an expanding demand more than offset the displacing power of the machine.

II

A large percentage of the hand compositors affected by the introduction of the linotype were members of the International Typographical Union. While this union enjoys the distinction of being the oldest national organization of trade-unionists in the United States, the subordinate unions were until the eighties almost inde-

8. The general opinion among printers and publishers appears to be that, in those newspaper offices which introduced linotypes about 1895, by the year 1900 the number of printers employed was as great as it was before the introduction of linotypes. See on this point, Report of Industrial Commission, vol. vii, p. 279 (Testimony of Mr. Donnelly, President of the International Typographical Union).

9. Quoted in The Typographical Journal, vol. viii, p. 204.

pendent of the national body. About 1888 the national body began to absorb power from the subordinate unions, but this movement went on slowly. To a considerable extent, therefore, the policy of the printers with reference to the machine was determined by the local unions. So large, however, were the interests evidently at stake that the local unions followed certain general lines of policy laid down by the national conventions and advised by the national executive board.[1]

At the thirty-sixth annual session of the International Typographical Union held in Kansas City in June, 1888, a resolution was adopted that "the International Typographical Union favors the recognition of such [typesetting] machines," and "recommends that subordinate unions . . . take speedy action looking to their recognition and regulation, endeavoring everywhere to secure their operation by union men upon a scale of wages which shall secure compensation equal to that paid hand compositors."[2] At that time less than 100 machines were in operation in the United States and Canada, and the greater part of these were being run experimentally.

By the time the session of 1889 was held, the growing importance of the question led to the formulation of the union's policy in a general rule, controlling the action of all subordinate unions. With unimportant changes in phraseology, this rule remained in force. In its original form, it read as follows: "The International Typographical Union directs that in all offices within its jurisdiction where typesetting machines are used, practical printers shall be employed to run them and also that subordinate unions shall regulate the scale of

1. The evident necessity for the adoption of a common machine policy was a powerful influence in hastening the movement toward centralization in the Typographical Union.

2. Report of Proceedings of the Thirty-Sixth Annual Session of the International Typographical Union, p. 181.

wages on such machines."[3] Curiously enough, the printers were at first reluctant to operate the machines and at the thirty-eighth session resolutions were adopted urging "that members of subordinate unions should learn to operate . . . machines wherever in use."[4]

By June of the next year, 1891, when the thirty-ninth annual session of the Typographical Union was held, the delegates were convinced of the grave importance of the machine question. In February, the subordinate union at Indianapolis had sent two of its members to New York to investigate at first hand the working of machines. The committee found that operators on the improved linotype were able to produce an average of 3,000 ems per hour, and believed a speed of 4,000 ems possible. They recommended that wages for operators should be on a time scale and that the hours of labor should be shorter than those prevailing for hand composition.[5] The report of this committee, published both as a pamphlet and in *The Typographical Journal*, exercised a large influence on the convention held in the following June. At that session a special committee on typesetting devices recommended "that a weekly or time scale be adopted for the operation of machines," and "that the hours of labor upon them be reduced to the lowest possible number — eight hours being the maximum."[6] It was urged that a time scale was more equitable than the piece system on account of the new-

3. Report of Proceedings of the Thirty-Seventh Annual Session of the International Typographical Union, 1889, p. 91.

4. Report of Proceedings of the Thirty-Eighth Annual Session of the International Typographical Union, 1890, p. 153.

5. Typesetting Machines. Report of an Inquiry into Their Merits and the General Situation surrounding them, made by Typographical Union No. 1, Indianapolis, Indiana.

6. Report of Proceedings of the Thirty-Ninth Annual Session of the International Typographical Union, p. 196.

ness of the work and the consequent difficulty of estimating the average output to be expected. The demand for a reduction in hours was based on the ground that "the work upon machines was of a more exhaustive character mentally and physically than hand composition." The recommendations of the committee were adopted and became binding on the subordinate unions. The strong feeling in the craft in favor of local autonomy secured the repeal of these two rules at the session of the International Union in 1893,[7] but they became the basis for practically all wage scales formed and the great majority of agreements for linotype operators provided for a time scale and an eight-hour day.

The machine policy of the union was thus based on the requirement that the machines should be operated only by journeymen printers. This rule had two distinct parts. In the first place, it asserted the claim that the operation of the machine was printer's work. Important as this part of the rule was in minimizing displacement, it involved no break in the former practice of the union, and in effect was simply an extension of jurisdiction over machine operators. A different phase of the rule was the prohibition against the operation of the machine by apprentices. The uniform custom of the International Typographical Union hitherto had been to consider any of the work in a printing office proper for an apprentice.

A slow movement toward the incorporation of machine work in the regular training of the apprentice began in 1893, when it was provided that "apprentices may work on machines in the last year of apprenticeship, who shall be paid two thirds of the wages of regular operators until their time of apprenticeship shall have

7. Report of Proceedings of the Forty-First Annual Session of the International Typographical Union, p. 201.

expired." [8] This rule was anomalous in two particulars; it restricted the time of learning the machine to a part of the apprenticeship period, and it formulated a wage scale for a class of apprentices. In both respects, the regulation was entirely opposed to the former practice of the union. The increasing use of machines and the rapid displacement of hand compositors led at the next session of the International Union to a reaction and to the withdrawal of this slight concession. The new enactment provided that "indentured apprentices may work on machine during the last six weeks of apprenticeship, providing they receive the scale of the subordinate union." [9] As very few apprentices in the printing trade have been indentured during recent years this modification of the prohibition was not important.

By a rule passed at the session of the Union in 1899, "regularly employed apprentices in machine offices" were "privileged to practise on machine during all of the last three months of their apprenticeship." [1] Since the product of apprentices who "practised" on machines could not be used by the employer, while any other part of their output had a market value, not many employers were likely to put apprentices during working hours at "practising" on machines. An apprentice by virtue of the rule might, however, acquire a small amount of knowledge out of working hours. It was not until 1903 that the union printers were willing to permit the machine product of apprentices to be used. The session of 1903 enacted that "regularly employed apprentices shall be privileged to work on machines during all of the

8. Proceedings of the Forty-First Annual Session of the International Typographical Union, p. 200.
9. Proceedings of the Forty-Second Session of the International Typographical Union, p. 31.
1. Report of the Proceedings of the Forty-Fifth Session of the International Typographical Union, p. 50.

last three months of their apprenticeship and the learners' scale shall apply to such apprentices." [2] This small relaxation was proposed and strongly urged by the executive committee of the International Union.

The Typographical Union was actuated by two motives in the enactment of legislation prohibiting the operation of machines by apprentices. The members felt strongly that as far as possible the opportunity to learn the new devices ought to be restricted to the displaced hand compositors. The apprentices had far greater adaptability than the displaced men, who, in the great majority of cases, must learn the machine or quit the trade. The slight modification in the restriction of machine work to journeymen in 1903 was due to the passing of the early stage in the introduction of the machine. The printer who had been displaced by the machine had either found his place in the trade or had abandoned it for some other occupation. The maintenance of the rule as modified was due to the strong fear that machine work might fall into the hands of men who are not printers. If the Typographical Union had been fully convinced that the operation of machines was neither practicable nor profitable except by journeymen printers trained in the trade as a whole, there would have been no reason for the continuance of any restriction on the operation of machines by apprentices.

In order to facilitate the policy of manning the machines with printers, the subordinate unions found it necessary to provide for journeymen an opportunity of learning the new device. Since a learner on the linotype produces for the first few weeks only a small amount of matter, employers required some concessions in wages during this period. The unions, usually after confer-

2. Report of the Proceedings of the Forty-Ninth Session of the International Typographical Union, p. 110.

ences with employers, formulated what were known as "learners' scales." The wages paid under these scales were lower than the regular wage for operators and the period of apprenticeship was limited. The International Union left the decision as to the terms of "learners' scales" entirely to the subordinate unions, except that from 1896 to 1898 the period of apprenticeship was fixed at two months.[3] The local unions showed themselves for the most part keenly alive to the importance of securing for their members a knowledge of the machine. The formulation of a "learners' scale" obviated the necessity of bringing expert operators from other cities and in so far as this was accomplished avoided the displacement which would have resulted from the transfer of operators from one city to another.

So important did the avoidance of local displacement appear to the union printers that they attempted in 1894 to strengthen the hands of local unions by a general rule, which required that "members of a subordinate union employed in an office at the time of the introduction of machines shall have preference as operators, one expert operator being allowed."[4] This rule only remained in force a short time. An appeal against its enforcement was taken to the International President by an expert operator who maintained that his rights as a member of the union were thereby infringed. President Prescott in the case of Wandress *vs.* San Francisco Typographical Union No. 21, sustained this contention on the ground that the rule was a violation of the constitution of the International Union, under which a member with a traveling card is entitled to the "friendship and good offices" of any union to which the card may be

3. Proceedings of the Forty-Third Session of the International Typographical Union.

4. Proceedings of the Forty-Second Annual Session of the International Typographical Union, p. 38.

presented.[5] Mr. Prescott was careful to point out that the rights of a traveling member would not be abridged where an employer "of his own volition or at the instigation of any person or persons decided to receive no application for situations until those who were working in his office had been given an opportunity to show their ability or inability to manipulate machines."[6] The burden of avoiding local displacement was thus placed entirely on the subordinate unions, and in the great majority of cases, agreements were concluded with employers by which their old employees were retained as machine operators.[7]

Several of the larger local unions went further in their anxiety to meet the demand for skilled operators. Machines were bought or rented and members were permitted to practise on them.[8] The introduction of machines was undoubtedly much facilitated by the constant efforts of the unions to supply the needed operators. The unions were actuated by a keen desire to control the machine and the fear that if the printers did not furnish the operators, they would be secured from some other source.

The subordinate unions frequently had to deal with propositions to decrease the scale for hand composition in order to enable employers to meet the competition of the machine. This matter was entirely within the jurisdiction of the subordinate unions, but the officials of the International Union strongly advised against any attempt to keep the machine out by cutting down the price

5. The Typographical Journal, vol. viii, p. 301.
6. Idem.
7. Some unions pursued a less far-sighted policy by refusing to grant reasonable "learners' scales," vide The Typographical Journal, vol. vi, No. 2, p. 3. The officials of the International Union constantly impressed upon the local unions the necessity of securing for their members an opportunity to learn the machine.
8. The Typographical Journal, vol. vi, No. 3, p. 7.

for hand work. In his address to the forty-second annual session, Mr. Prescott said "Those familiar with the productiveness of machines are agreed that hand work cannot begin to compete with them, and it is therefore futile to attempt to stay the tide of their introduction by a reduction in the scale unless we are prepared to suffer level decreases amounting to 40 to 50 per cent, and at that figure a better living could be secured at almost any unskilled vocation. A serious reduction in the rate of hand composition is sure to affect the machine scale also." [9] Notwithstanding this eminently sane advice, as the hand compositors saw themselves displaced, some of them turned to their only weapon of defense — competition with the machine.[1] One method was for a group of compositors to form a partnership and furnish matter ready set to publishers at a price as low as that formerly paid for composition in the publishers' offices. The compositors paid their own rent, their fuel and light bills, as well as the cost of type. The scale of the union was thus underbid by its own members. Another practice much in vogue in small cities was for a number of displaced compositors to print on a coöperative plan a small newspaper. Assisted by the sympathy of the community, they were able in some cases to make a living wage.[2] The unions in common decency could hardly deal harshly with such covert methods of competition, but the union scales for hand composition were rarely lowered for the purpose of competing with the machine.

Of direct opposition to the introduction of the machine, there was practically none. Occasionally a small

9. Report of Proceedings of the Forty-Second Annual Session of the International Typographical Union, p. 3.

1. The Typographical Journal, vol. vi, No. 22, p. 1. Ibid., vol. x, p. 251 and p. 342. Ibid., vol. xi, p. 304.

2. The Typographical Journal, vol. vi, No. 5, p. 7 and No. 20, p. 3.

union refused for a time to make a scale for machines, but the International Union steadily discountenanced such a policy, and since the subordinate unions could not legally declare a strike without the sanction of the executive board of the International Union, they were soon persuaded to adopt a different line of conduct.[3] The Kansas printers were able to keep the machine out of the State printing office for a time by political influence.[4] But in general, the printers acquiesced in the new order of things without a struggle.

During the years 1894–96, many printers were unable to secure work. The depression of business intensified the distress occasioned by the introduction of the machine. No safe estimate can be made of the extent of unemployment among printers at this time, but some indication is furnished by the fact that the Germania Typographia, the national union of the German printers, with a membership of about 1,300, paid $17,262.50 [5] in out-of-work benefits during the fiscal year 1893–94. Twenty per cent of its members were unemployed in October, 1893.[6] The proportion of unemployed among the members of the Typographical Union was not nearly so large, but it was undoubtedly very great.

The International Typographical Union has never paid an out-of-work benefit, but has relied for the relief of unemployed members on the sharing of work. In former periods of industrial depression, members without regular employment had been given a part of the work controlled by their more fortunate fellow unionists. The desire to facilitate the sharing of work had led to

3. Proceedings of the Forty-Third Session of the International Typographical Union, p. 27.
4. The Typographical Journal, vol. x, p. 453.
5. 25-jahrige Geschichte der Deutsch-Amerikanischen Typographia, von Hugo Miller, p. 58.
6. Ibid., p. 45.

the building up of an elaborate set of rules constituting what is known among union printers as the "substitute system." In the first few years of the introduction of the machine this system gave temporary relief to the unemployed, and as machines were installed the displaced compositors flocked into the remaining hand offices as substitutes. The continual decrease in the number of hand offices added to the number of substitutes and diminished their opportunities for securing employment. The unemployed were chiefly workmen of advanced age, who were unable to operate machines at sufficient speed. They could not secure employment in other branches of the trade because they had become highly specialized in the setting of straight matter. Some of them went to the smaller towns to which the machine had not come; others abandoned the printing industry.

Even if the International Union had had an adequate system of out-of-work benefits, it is doubtful if this class of compositors would have been materially helped. Their retention in the printing trade was an impossibility, and the inevitable readjustment could be made better at an earlier time than after a period of precarious livelihood made possible by benefits. Other printers were only temporarily displaced and with the revival of business and the enlargement of demand found places in the trade. The large local unions exerted themselves to tide their unfortunate members over the period of depression. In several cities, the number of days which any member might work in a week was limited to five, in order that the substitute system might afford relief for larger numbers.

III

The most pronounced economic advantage accruing to the printers from the introduction of the machine was the material reduction secured in the length of the working day. Certain peculiar trade conditions favored the Typographical Union in its demand for a short working day on machines. The machine was first introduced in newspaper offices, and the number of machines in newspaper offices has always far exceeded the number in book and job offices. The following table gives the number of machines in use in each class of offices for the years 1901, 1902 and 1904:[7]

	1901	1902	1904
Book and job offices	837	981	1,638
Newspaper offices	4,138	4,834	5,491

The requirements of the newspaper office consequently were an important factor in setting the length of the working day on machines. Prior to the introduction of the linotype, wages for hand compositors in newspaper offices had been almost uniformly on a piece basis, the union scale regulating the price per thousand ems set. The unions required the publishers to give employment for a fixed minimum number of hours each working day. The maximum working day had never been a matter of concern to the unions so far as newspaper offices were concerned. The stress had always been the other way, since the publishers were desirous of keeping in their employ as large a number of printers as possible in order that any sudden strain might be met. The printers, with many local variations, had adopted the rule that six or seven hours' work must be furnished each day. Allowing for time spent in distribution of type and in

7. Compiled from returns made to the Secretary of the International Typographical Union, vide The Typographical Journal, vol. xviii, No. 11 (supplement); ibid., vol. xxiv, No. 2, p. 212.

pasting up "dupes," the usual working day on newspapers was rarely less than ten hours.

Newspaper publishers always need the largest composing force during the last few hours before the paper goes to press. In a peculiar sense it is true in newspaper work that the productivity of a workman is not reduced proportionately with a decrease in the length of the working day. The cheapness of machine composition made it possible for publishers to increase the capacity of their force in order to secure a much desired increase in effectiveness during the last hours. The proposal of the union for an eight-hour day on machine composition therefore met with small opposition from the employers.

The following table shows the length of the working week for machine operators in offices controlled by the Typographical Union, according to scales in force January 1, 1904: [8]

Number of hours constituting a week's work	Morning Newspaper Offices	Evening Newspaper Offices	Weekly Newspaper Offices	Book and Job Offices	Total
Unions reporting less than 48 hours	48	38	11	18	115
Unions reporting 48 hours	266	296	199	193	934
Unions reporting more than 48 and less than 54 hours	15	37	38	23	113
Unions reporting 54 hours	53	139	93	86	371
Unions reporting more than 54 hours	1	0	0	2	3

Of 1,536 scales for operators in the various kinds of machine offices, 68 per cent fixed forty-eight hours or less as the maximum working week. The proportion of operators having a forty-eight hour week was still greater, since the larger unions usually have shorter working days than the smaller ones. The relatively

8. Compiled from returns made to the Secretary of the International Typographical Union, vide The Typographical Journal, vol. xxiv, No. 2, p. 211.

large number of scales for evening newspaper offices fixing more than forty-eight hours as the maximum working week, was due to the fact that many small towns have evening newspapers and no morning newspapers. It is probable that between 80 and 90 per cent of the union machine operators in the country had in 1904 a maximum working week of forty-eight hours or less. In the larger cities the length of the working day was usually the same on morning and evening newspapers, while it was somewhat longer on weekly newspapers and in book and job offices. The other printers employed in the composing rooms of the newspaper profited by the reduction in the hours of machine compositors. "Admen," "floormen," proof readers and hand compositors employed in machine offices usually enjoyed the short working day of their co-laborers, the operators, who set the hours of labor for the entire composing room.

The effect of the machine on wages is difficult to estimate on account of the change in the method of payment from the piece to the time system. The following table gives for each of the ten largest cities in the United States, the union scale for hand composition in 1891 and the union scale for machine operators in 1904.[9]

Assuming that a hand compositor was able on the average to set 1,000 ems per hour, the wages per hour of machine operators in 1904 were about 20 per cent higher than those of hand compositors in 1891. Since, however, the hand compositor worked ten hours as against the operator's eight, the day wages for the two kinds of work do not differ materially. A simple comparison of the union scales for the two classes of workmen neglects,

9. This table is compiled from reports made to the Secretary of the International Union, vide Proceedings, 1892, p. 204 et seq., and The Typographical Journal, vol. xxiv, No. 2, p. 213 et seq.

	Union scales for hand composition per 1000 ems, in 1891		Union scales for machine operators per week in 1904		Number of hours constituting a week for machine operators	Wages of machine operators per hour	
	Day work	Night work	Day work	Night work		Day work	Night work
New York	40c.	50c.	$24	$27	48	50c.	$56\frac{1}{4}$c.
Chicago.........	41	46	24	26.40	48	50	55
Philadelphia....	40	40	20	25	48	$41\frac{2}{3}$	$52\frac{1}{12}$
St. Louis	38	43	23.25	26.10	46	$50\frac{25}{46}$	$56\frac{17}{23}$
Boston	38	45	22.36	24.36	42	53	58
Baltimore......	40	45	21	22.50	42	50	$53\frac{1}{2}$
Cleveland......	40	43	21	24	48	$43\frac{2}{3}$	50
Buffalo.........	33	35	19.50	22.50	42	$46\frac{3}{7}$	$53\frac{4}{7}$
San Francisco ..	45	50	27	30	45	60	$66\frac{2}{3}$
Cincinnati	41	45	22	25	48	$45\frac{5}{6}$	$52\frac{1}{12}$
Average	39.6	44.2				51	57

however, an important consideration. Under the piece system few employers paid any of their workmen more than the minimum rate, while a considerable part of the machine operators in all the cities included in the table received more than the scale.[1] The speedy and accurate operator was paid a differential wage over the slower workman.[2] Machine operators, in these cities, therefore received somewhat more on the average for eight hours' work than hand compositors did at the introduction of the linotype for ten hours' work. The difference in favor of the operator was even greater in the smaller cities.

Regularity of employment was far greater among the machine operators than it had been among the hand compositors as a class. The constant expansion in the

1. In the arbitration proceedings held in June, 1903, to determine the wage scale for machine operators in New York City, the New York Union laid stress on the fact that one half of the newspaper operators in that city received more than the existing scale. (Arbitration Proceedings, Typographical Union, No. 6 vs. New York Newspaper Publishers — MS.)

2. In Chicago, a bonus was paid in 1904 to all operators on matter set beyond a fixed amount. In the other cities, the differential was not fixed so exactly but worked itself out by individual bargaining.

demand for operators kept the competent workmen fully employed. The "learners' scales" were so arranged that employers trained new operators only when they were needed. The machine, moreover, increased indirectly but materially the regularity of employment for all printers through its effect on the number of apprentices. As long as straight matter was set by hand, there was a profit to the employer in having apprentices, since within a comparatively short time they became proficient enough in this branch of the trade to more than repay the employer for the low wages paid them. The result was that the number of apprentices was out of proportion to the growth of the industry. Largely as a result of the overcrowding in the trade, a class of printers came into existence who were known as "tramp" printers. Drifting here and there in search of work, many of them acquired dissolute habits. Printers holding regular situations were expected to share work with these fellow unionists, and in many cities, it became the custom for unmarried newspaper compositors to work only two or three days each week during periods of depression.

The first convention of the Journeymen Printers of the United States held in 1850 was strongly of the opinion that "too many printers had been manufactured of late years." [3] The local printers' unions had always put forward as one of their chief aims, the restriction of the number of apprentices, but had achieved only a very partial success. The introduction of the machine appreciably diminished the importance of the apprenticeship question to the printers. Since straight composition was the branch of the work to which the machine was best suited, the profit from apprentices

3. Proceedings of the National Convention of Journeymen Printers of the United States, New York, December 2, 1850. Philadelphia, 1851.

sensibly decreased, and the future needs of the business became the controlling factor in the regulation of the number of apprentices. The "tramp" printer, a sign of an unhealthy trade condition, had by 1904 almost disappeared and confined his operations to the smaller towns in which hand composition still maintained its hold.

Besides the length of the working day, the rate of pay and regularity of employment, one other factor in the conditions of work is worthy of attention in every trade — the intensity of labor required. Linotype operators are universally agreed that the high speed attained on the machines makes the work far more exhausting than hand composition. The International Typographical Union at times went close to limitation of output in its desire to keep the speed required within what the union consider reasonable limits. At the forty-first annual session it was enacted that "no member . . . shall be allowed to accept work . . . where a task, stint, or dead line is imposed by the employer on operators of typesetting devices." [4] The same session prohibited operators from accepting a "bonus per thousand above the regular scale." [5] The fear that the employers would raise the required amount so high as to make the work a very heavy strain or that through the incentive of a bonus the standard would be put up by especially skillful operators to a point difficult of attainment, led to the enactment of these laws.

The prohibition on the payment of bonus was repealed in 1894,[6] but the sentiment against this form of wages remained very strong, and in 1902 it was enacted that no bonus should be accepted by machine

4. Proceedings of the Forty-First Annual Session of the International Typographical Union, p. 200.
5. Ibid., p. 201.
6. Ibid., p. 38.

operators where "such bonus is voluntary on the part of the employer and is not provided for in the scale of prices."[7] The session of 1902 went much farther than any of its predecessors and recommended "that subordinate unions establish a stated amount of machine composition which is considered a fair day's work."[8] The rules of the Typographical Union, if they had been literally enforced as they stood in 1902, denied the employer the right to place any definite stint, but gave the union the right to do the very thing prohibited to employers. Despite the prohibition against employers' fixing the accomplishment of a fixed amount of work as a condition of employment, this was done in nearly all newspaper offices, and in 1903 the Typographical Union repealed its prohibition.[9] The same session struck out the section recommending the "establishment by the local unions of a fair day's work."[1] The rule against the acceptance of bonus except when paid according to the union scale was the only remaining rule of this kind in 1904, except a provision that "members shall not engage in speed contests."[2] The purpose of this unique prohibition was to prevent exaggerated ideas arising of the amount proper for an operator to perform.

Such rules as those described were entirely ineffective in checking the increase in the speed of operators. Occasionally a local union sheltered an unreasonable demand behind such rules, but in the main, the speed of the operator was determined only by his ability. The large number of operators receiving more than the minimum wage scale in 1904 indicates that as a class

7. Proceedings of the Forty-Eighth Session of the International Typographical Union, p. 141.
8. Ibid., p. 142.
9. Ibid., p. 123.
1. Ibid., p. 136.
2. International Typographical Book of Laws, 1903, General Laws, sec. 69.

their output was not arbitrarily limited. A large part of the supporters of the legislation described desired to secure by this means employment for operators who were not able to reach the standard set. The constant increase in the speed of the operator had made the old provisions for learning the machine inadequate. The proper remedy was for the unions and employers to revise the "learners' scales" to conform to existing conditions.

IV

The success of the International Typographical Union in enforcing the rule that printers shall be employed as linotype operators has been frequently attributed solely to the strength of that organization. In his testimony before the Industrial Commission, Mr. Gompers, the President of the American Federation of Labor, said: "The printers have had a remarkable history, particularly within the last five years. The machine . . . was introduced and it is one of the cases where a new machine revolutionizing a whole trade was introduced that did not involve a wholesale disaster even for a time, and it is due to the fact that the International Typographical Union has grown to be an organized factor and recognized by those employing printers as a factor to be considered."[3] A more explicit statement of the same view was made before the Commission by Mr. D. F. Kennedy, an organizer of the Federation of Labor for Indiana. He said: "These [typecasting] machines would now be run by typewriters, not typesetters, had it not been for the union taking possession of the situation to the extent that they compelled them to use typesetters to run the machine."[4]

3. Report of the Industrial Commission, vol. vii, p. 615.
4. Ibid., vol. vii, p. 748.

If a union can force in every period of machine introduction the preferential employment of its members on the new devices, at least a partial solution of the problem of the displaced workman is offered. The introduction of machinery frequently leads to the employment of less highly trained and less skillful workmen; in many cases to the replacing of skilled artisans with poorly paid women and children operatives. The printers required an apprenticeship of four years before the workman was permitted to operate the linotype. How far is it true that the Typographical Union by sheer force of combination has been able to force the employment of highly paid workmen to perform work which might be done by a much cheaper class of laborers? On the answer to this question depends the decision as to the possibility of similar combinations of workmen in other trades utilizing the experience of the printers on those occasions when fundamental reconstructions of their trades are in progress. A policy which requires the employment of skilled workmen for work easily within the power of less skillful employees would be clearly uneconomic, and its continued enforcement would be against great economic pressure.

The International Typographical Union undoubtedly occupied an advantageous strategic position in the introduction of the machine. Its chief strength for many years had consisted in the control of the greater part of the larger newspaper offices. It is entirely probable that the union did secure the control of the machine in some of these offices because the publishers feared the boycott, which is peculiarly effective against newspapers. A second advantage possessed by the Union lay in the fact that as the machine was introduced in the smaller newspaper and job offices, the supply of expert workmen trained in the offices of the large union newspapers furnished a ready labor market for the employers installing linotypes.

Several facts point, however, to the conclusion that the policy of the printers did not succeed simply through the power of combination. In the early years of the introduction of the linotype much was said about the possibility of operating machines with unskilled labor.[5] The experiment was tried in several cities, but with such small success that employers abandoned the attempt to recruit their linotype operators from this class of labor. Non-union offices with substantial uniformity employed printers as machine operators. The union rules did not bind these employers and their policy was dictated by economic interest. The same practice prevailed in all other countries where the linotype was introduced.[6] No tendency to replace male with female labor appeared. In January, 1904, the number of women operating typesetting and typecasting machines in the United States and Canada was 520, about 5 per cent of the total number of operators.[7] The number of women engaged in the United States in 1900 as printers and compositors was 15,875,[8] about 15 per cent of the total number of printers and compositors.

A trade-union rule without economic justification would probably have won its chief success at the outset. The returns made to the officers of the Typographical Union show that so far from the union's losing control of the machine, the proportion of union to non-union operators increased from 1901 to 1904. The following

5. The printers were profoundly affected by the fear that they would be supplanted by a cheaper class of labor. The continuance of the restriction on apprentices working the machine was due, as has been noted, to the persistence of this fear.

6. See Webb, Industrial Democracy, p. 407; Radiguer, Maitres Imprimeurs et Ouvriers Typographes, p. 482.

7. The Typographical Journal, vol. xxiv, No. 2, p. 212.

8. Twelfth Census of the United States, Population, part 11, p. 507.

table shows by years the percentage of union operators and machine tenders.[9] In 1904, 92¾ per cent of all machine employees according to these returns were members of the union.[1] In no other branch of the trade did the union control so large a proportion of the workmen.

	Percentage of total number		
	1901	1902	1904
Male Machine Operators	92	92	94¼
Female Machine Operators	63	56	62½
Machine Tenders	86	89	95
Operator Machinists	100	90	93

A consideration of the technical character of the linotype confirms the conclusion that it differs from many machines in requiring for its most profitable operation the skill of the superseded handicraftsman. The amount produced on a linotype is directly proportional to the skill of the operator, while many labor-saving inventions reduce the work of the laborer to that of tending the machine. Every part of the hand compositor's knowledge is useful to the machine operator, except an acquaintance with the location of the case boxes, and instead the operator must learn the keyboard of the machine. In addition, the operator must think far more quickly. He must not only know the same things, but he must be able to use his knowledge more rapidly.

The real merit of the policy of the Typographical Union was that it secured for its members an opportunity to show to the employer that the printer was more profitable than the unskilled workman as a machine operator. This policy required the frank recognition of the machine, its honest working and fair concessions to employers during the period of machine apprenticeship.

9. Compiled from The Typographical Journal, vol. xviii, No. 11 (supplement); ibid., vol. xxiv, No. 2, p. 212.

1. The census made by the union officials omitted more non-unionists but the conclusion as to the tendency is not weakened by such omissions.

CHAPTER II

THE STONECUTTERS' UNION AND THE STONE-PLANER

SUMMARY

The development of the machine, 30. — I. The displacement of labor involved, 33. — II. The policy of the stonecutters' union with reference to the use of the stone-planer, 35. — The formation and activities of "dual" unions in the trade, 52. — III. The effect of the machine on the conditions of employment of hand cutters, 59.

MACHINES for planing stone have been used for many years. The original machines were simply iron-planers slightly reconstructed, and were worked by a gear-and-rack drive. They were successful in planing flaggings and other paving material for which a smooth surface was not required, but could not be used on building material. About 1880 a new type of planer was designed, in which a screw was substituted for the gear-and-rack drive. A regular motion was thus attained, and the machine became a practicable means of working building stone. It was possible, not only to plane stone on the machine, but also by the use of various forms of edges to cut moldings of any ordinary design. A large part of this work had formerly been done by skilled stonecutters using chisel and hammer. The planer, however, by no means entirely replaced the stonecutter. It was still necessary to employ stonecutters to do much that the machine could not do. Also, it was cheaper to do small pieces by hand than to mount them on the planer.

The new planers were introduced almost simultaneously in the Bedford limestone district, in the New

York bluestone region, and in New York City. Planers were not much used, however, until about 1895; from 1895 to 1900 they were rapidly introduced in the Bedford limestone region, and by 1915 they had become a necessary part of stone-working equipment in all parts of the United States. The great increase from 1895 to 1915 in the use of the planer on building stone was closely connected with the rapid development of the Bedford limestone industry.[1] Planers were used in 1915 on all varieties of building stone except granite and some kinds of sandstone; but they were first extensively employed on Bedford limestone, and were still most advantageously employed on that material.

The widening use of Bedford limestone as a building material made it desirable for stone contractors to keep in stock quantities of unfinished Bedford limestone. Wherever a contractor was cutting a large amount of this material he found it profitable to install a planer. On the other hand, when a large building was to be erected, it was frequently more economical to have the stone prepared as far as possible at or near the quarries. There were thus two distinct fields for the use of the planer: first, at or near the quarries,[2] and, second, in local stoneyards.

When the planers were first introduced much was said about the injury they did to the stone, and it was asserted that planed stone soon disintegrated.[3] The strong desire of some of the workmen to discredit the

1. From 1900 to 1910, the value of the annual quarry output of Bedford limestone increased from $1,639,985 to $3,106,520, although in the same period the production of building stone in the United States, exclusive of granite, increased only from $7,439,000 to $10,506,543 (Mineral Resources of the United States, Part II, 1910, pp. 645, 649, 673).

2. In 1909 there were eighty-four planers in the Bedford district (J. A. Udden, "The Oölitic Limestone Industry at Bedford and Bloomington, Indiana," in Bulletin 430, U. S. Geological Survey).

3. See Stone, September and October, 1898.

machines induced them to exaggerate the injury done.[4] A writer in the *Stone Cutters' Journal* for March, 1893, declared that the surface of planed stone rotted and the projections fell off. It has long been understood in the trade that planer-cut stone is fully as durable as that cut by hand if the planing is properly done, but that the planer may be made to run so deep as to "bruise" the stone.

The first planers were slow and required a large amount of power, but they were soon much improved in both respects by changes in the form of the drive. The early screw drive was gradually replaced by a worm or a spiral drive. The newer forms of the machine saved from 50 to 60 per cent in power, and attained a much higher speed. The efficiency of the planer was also increased by various modifications in its form. From about 1900, planers were made with a divisible bed, by means of which the output of a planer on small blocks was doubled. Two planermen were necessary, but the overhead charges were cut in half. Later, also, planers were introduced which would cut stone of circular form.

The present chapter deals with the effect of the introduction of the planer on the stonecutters. In the following sections, the displacement caused by the machine, the policy adopted by the stonecutters' union with reference to the planer, and the effect on the wages and hours of the hand workers will be considered. The period covered is from 1900 to 1915. By the latter date, the period of introduction may be regarded as concluded.

4. See, for example, a letter in the Stone Cutters' Journal, November, 1903, p. 10, in which the writer, the secretary of a local stonecutters' union, naïvely says: "Speaking about machine-cut stone reminds me that recently I read that a building in some part of Pennsylvania was crumbling or wasting so fast that oil of some kind was used on its face to preserve it. I think a southern stone was used from Florida. If we could ascertain that it was cut by machinery, what a splendid lever we would have in condemning cut stone."

I

The amount of labor saved by the use of a planer is difficult to estimate, since the advantage over handwork is largely relative to the class of stone and the kind of cutting. A single-platen planer of improved type when engaged on the work in which the planer is most superior to handwork in 1915 would do about as much work in an hour as ten stonecutters. The number of planers in use on building stone in the United States in 1915 was about 1,000.[5] Each of these probably did, on an average, an amount of work which would have required seven or eight stonecutters. The stone-planers in operation in the United States in that year on building stone, therefore, did an amount of work which would have required seven or eight thousand hand cutters.

Such statistical data as are available[6] indicate that the saving of labor made by the planer was not offset by any increase in the production of stone, and that therefore the displacement of labor was equal to the amount of labor saved. The reports of the United States Geological Survey on the production of stone estimate as follows the value of the exterior building stone, other than granite, produced in the United States:[7]

1900	$7,400,000
1905	12,900,000
1910	10,200,000
1913	8,274,786
1914	8,848,234

In the later years, a much larger part of the stone was

5. It is impossible to ascertain exactly the number of planers manufactured, since the machines are made by a number of manufacturers and the records of some of these are not available. The estimate made here is based on data supplied by the more important makers.

6. The Census of Occupations lumps together stonecutters, granite-cutters, and interior-marble cutters. In 1900 there were 54,460 "stonecutters" in the United States; in 1910 the number was 35,737. The Census warns, however, that these figures are not comparable.

7. Mineral Resources of the United States, passim.

finished at the quarries, and such stone had a higher value. The amount of exterior building stone produced was, therefore, probably less in 1915 than in 1900.

As in the case of all inventions of labor-saving machinery, except where monopolized, the planer brought substantial reductions in the price of the commodity. In the late eighteen-eighties Bedford stone was set in Chicago at $1.85 per cubic foot. In 1913 the price was $1.12½. Similar reductions were made in the price of marble and of those sandstones which could be cut by the planer. That these reductions did not lead to an increased use of stone was due to the active competition of concrete and terra cotta as building materials. Concrete rivaled stone chiefly as material for bridges. The increasing use of terra cotta was largely due to the cheapness with which a scheme of building decoration in which the same ornament is repeated a number of times can be executed in terra cotta. The inroads made by terra cotta and concrete from 1900 to 1915 upon the field formerly regarded as preëmpted by stone would have been greater if a reduction in the cost of cut stone had not been made possible by the introduction of the planer.

In the period from 1900 to 1915 the use of other labor-saving devices besides the planer was much extended in the stone trade. Pneumatic tools and diamond-pointed saws took over much of the stonecutter's work. It may be roughly estimated that in 1900 there were between 20,000 and 25,000 stonecutters in the United States. The labor-saving devices introduced in the trade, chiefly after 1900, did in 1915 an amount of work which, at the lowest estimate, would have required the labor of 10,000 hand cutters.[8] By 1915, probably one half of the stonecutters had been displaced from the trade.

8. A competent authority informs the writer that the number of stonecutters in New York and its vicinity in 1900 was 2,100, and in 1910, 1,000.

II

The workmen engaged in cutting marble, limestone, and sandstone for use in the exterior of buildings are known as stonecutters, or sometimes, to distinguish them from the granite-cutters, as soft-stone cutters or freestone cutters. Besides the stonecutters, workmen of one other trade, the marble-cutters, who are employed chiefly in cutting and finishing stone intended for interior decoration, were displaced by the planer. But the marble-cutters were a relatively small and poorly organized group, and never adopted any definite policy with regard to the operation of the planers. In studying trade-union policy with reference to the introduction of the planer it will be possible, therefore, to confine attention to the stonecutters.

The stonecutters were one of the first trades in the United States to organize a national union. Copies of an official journal of the Journeymen Stone Cutters' Association of the United States of America, with dates as early as 1853, are extant. But the national unions of the stonecutters have always been decentralized in structure. As a result, one after another has gone to pieces. The present national union — the Journeymen Stone Cutters' Association of North America, ordinarily known as the General Union, or more briefly as the G. U. — was organized in 1888.

In considering the policy of the stonecutters with reference to the planer, the weakness of the national union must always be borne in mind. During the period under review the governing body of the General Union, between conventions held at irregular intervals, was an executive board, which was called together only in grave emergencies. The only beneficiary feature of the national union was a death benefit of from $50 to $150, according to length of membership. Until 1913 strike benefits were paid only after being voted upon by the branches. The annual dues of the national union until 1913 were only twenty-five cents per month, and in any considerable strike the funds were soon exhausted. The local organizations of stonecutters frequently severed their connection with the national union, which was powerless to restrain them. It was the rule rather than the exception for the local bodies in the largest cities to maintain their independence of the General Union.[9]

Until 1895 the stonecutters did not concern themselves about the planer. The number of planers in use was small, and they were to be found chiefly at the quarries, where the stonecutters were either unorganized or organized in independent local unions. The first impulse to the formulation of a national policy was given by the attempts first to control and later to prohibit the use of the planer, inaugurated in 1895 by the Chicago local union of stonecutters.

The use of planers in Chicago began about 1892. The local union in 1895 asked unsuccessfully for the insertion, in the agreement with the Chicago cut-stone contractors, of provisions limiting the hours during which the machines were to be operated, and requiring that the planers should be operated by union men. In January, 1896, the union insisted that the planers should not run more than eight hours a day, and a strike ensued.[1] The strike was settled by an agreement made on April 15.

9. Among the stonecutters an unaffiliated local organization is referred to as a "local union," while an affiliated organization is known as a "branch."

1. See Bogart, "The Chicago Building Trades Dispute," in Commons, Trade Unionism and Labor Problems, p. 110; testimony of J. Sullivan, chairman of Chicago Stone Cutters' Union, in Report of the Industrial Commission, vol. viii, p. 447; of Professor Graham Taylor, ibid., p. 542; of Mr. G. P. Gubbins, ibid., p. 221; Special Report of the Commissioner of Labor on Regulation and Restriction of Output, p. 350.

The planers were to be operated only eight hours a day and six days a week, and the laborers employed as planermen were to be replaced, in part immediately, and by degrees entirely, with stonecutters. The union in return agreed not to work on any stone which had been planed outside of Chicago, and "to keep out all stonework not planed or cut in Chicago."[2]

In 1898 the Chicago union demanded that for every planer operated the contractor should employ at least four stonecutters with hammer and chisel. The actual proportion in most of the yards was far below this, and the contractors refused to accede. After a strike of ten weeks a compromise was effected under which the contractors agreed to employ two stonecutters for every single planer and four stonecutters for every double planer. In January, 1899, the union notified the contractors that they would not work after April 1 in any yard where machinery, except saws and rubbing beds, was used. The contractors secured an extension of time to June 1, but on that date all the planers in Chicago stopped. The value of the machinery thrown out of use was estimated at over $100,000. Planers were not used in Chicago from June 1, 1899, until after the building-trades strike of 1900.

The gradual development of a machine policy in Chicago was naturally a matter of profound interest to the branches of the General Union, altho the Chicago union was an independent organization. At each stage in the struggle against the planer the Chicago union set forth its aims in letters to the *Stone Cutters' Journal*, the official organ of the General Union,[3] and urged the

2. See Stone Cutters' Journal, June, 1899, pp. 2, 11, 13; testimony of Henry Struble, in Report of the Industrial Commission, vol. viii, p. 356, and of J. Sullivan, ibid., p. 447.

3. See, for example, Stone Cutters' Journal, February, 1896, pp. 2, 13; May, 1899, p. 15; June, 1899, p. 15; July, 1899, p. 11.

inauguration of a general campaign against the planer. Editorials commending the course of the Chicago union appeared frequently in the *Journal*.[4] A number of branches of the General Union followed the example of the Chicago union in imposing restrictions on the operation of the planer. Thus in March, 1896, the Fort Wayne, Indiana, branch struck to limit the hours the planer might be worked and to require the employment of a stonecutter as planerman. In July, 1899, the Scranton branch forced the employment of stonecutters as planermen. In August, 1899, the St. Louis branch demanded that planers should not be run after October 1. The New York local union in 1901 required the employment of five hand cutters for each planer.

During the period from 1896 to 1900 a beginning was also made by the local organizations in another form of restriction: the prohibition of the shipment of planer-cut stone into cities where the local union was opposed to its use. Restriction on the shipment of hand-cut stone had long been enforced by the stonecutters. The earliest constitution of the General Union contained the following rule: "This Association will not countenance the transportation of cut stone from one place to another unless the wages and hours are equal; except in such cases where the interchange of work between two branches is mutually agreeable without regard to wages or hours." [5] The purpose of this provision was to prevent the competition of branches with low wage scales

4. See, for instance, Stone Cutters' Journal, May, 1896, p. 2; June, 1899, p. 2. In the issue of June, 1899, an editorial concluded as follows: "The planers are gone and we are glad; also that Chicago was the union that accomplished it. The men in Chicago are entitled to a world of credit for their aggressiveness and progressiveness. Chicago stonecutters have the honor to be the first union to secure the eight-hour day, the Saturday half-holiday, and now the abolition of the planer."

5. Constitution and By-Laws of the Journeymen Stone Cutters' Association of North American, 1892, Art. XIII.

and inferior working conditions. In certain of the larger places, notably New York and Chicago, by agreements between the stonecutters' unions and the contractors, the shipment of cut stone into the city had been forbidden entirely, without regard to whether wages and hours were lower in the shipping branch.

Planer-cut stone had been excluded from some localities on the ground that the working conditions at the shipping-point were inferior to those at the place of erection, but about 1896 a number of branches in which there were no planers began to exclude all planer-cut stone. In March, 1897, for instance, the Columbus, Ohio, branch decided not to permit any cut or planed stone to be shipped into Columbus. In 1899 a considerable quantity of marble was cut and planed at Tate, Georgia, for use in a Chicago building. The Chicago union refused to work on this marble, and by the aid of the Building Trades Council was able to secure its exclusion.[6] The Chicago local union also complained to the executive board of the General Union. The board was unanimous in holding that it was highly desirable that planed stone should not be shipped into cities where the planer was not in use, but realized that the rule of the General Union concerning the shipment of stone did not cover the case.[7]

The opposition to the planer increased so rapidly that in January, 1900, the executive board of the General Union was called into session. As a result of their deliberations, the members of the board determined to add to the constitution of the General Union two new rules: (1) "Planer work will not be permitted to be shipped into any city where the union has succeeded in

6. See testimony of F. P. Bagley, in Report of the Industrial Commission, vol. viii, p. 390.

7. Stone Cutters' Journal, September, 1899, pp. 9, 11; October, 1899, p. 11.

abolishing them"; (2) "Branches shall make every effort possible to prevent the introduction of planers in their jurisdiction." [8] Certain members of the board felt that these rules were insufficient to meet the situation, and proposed a rule forbidding any member of the union to work in a shop where a planer was in use, but the majority felt that so drastic a rule could not be enforced.

Of the two new rules adopted, the rule restricting the shipment of planer-cut stone was far the more important. It was modified from time to time, but remained in force from 1900 until 1908. It will be convenient, therefore, to neglect the strict chronology of events and, before taking account of other rules relating to the planer, to trace the operation of this rule through its entire history.

The adoption of the rule against the shipment of planer-cut stone was a popular measure, not merely because it promised to check the displacement of hand cutters, but also because it was in accord with the view that the stonecutters in each place should do the stonecutting of that place. The shipment of stone ready to go into the building had been greatly increased by the introduction of the planer, since the cutting could, in many cases, be done more cheaply at the shipping-points.

For the enforcement of the rule, the union relied chiefly on the coöperation of the branches at the shipping-points.[9] These branches were expected at least to refuse to do the necessary handwork on planed stone intended for places in which there were no planers, even if they did not go the length of striking against the

8. Stone Cutters' Journal, February, 1900, Supplement, p. 15.

9. Strictly construed, the rule protected only those cities which had succeeded in abolishing planers; but the executive board held that the rule also applied to cities in which planers had never been in use (Stone Cutters' Journal, March, 1901, pp. 5–8).

planing of the stone. The branches at the place of erection would, of course, refuse to finish stone worked on the planers. The union also placed some reliance on the fact that in certain places its members had control of the setting of stone. These workmen could be counted upon to refuse to set planed stone. The aid of the contractors was also hoped for. It was believed that the agreements in Chicago and New York which excluded cut stone showed that the contractors favored a policy of local protection. This would be the case particularly, it was thought, in those cities in which the contractors had no planers.

The coöperation of the shipping branches was given only grudgingly and partially. The self-interest of these branches led them to finish planer-cut stone intended for shipment unless it was clear that they would thereby involve themselves in difficulties with the General Union. As a result, the pages of the *Stone Cutters' Journal* from 1900 to 1908 teem with the accusations and the rejoinders of the branches. In March, 1901, for instance, the branch at Syracuse, New York, complained that planer-cut stone was being shipped to Syracuse from Gouverneur, New York. The Gouverneur branch replied that it had not known where the stone was to be used and that the work was finished. This form of defense was frequently used by the branches at the shipping-points. The branch at the place of erection, therefore, was forced to find out for itself where the work was being done, and usually by the time it had this information the branch at the shipping-point announced regretfully that the work was completed. Even where the branch at the shipping-point was willing to coöperate in preventing a shipment, the contractor was frequently able to conceal the destination of the stone.

The reliance of the stonecutters on their control of setting proved equally unwarranted. For many years there had been a dispute between the bricklayers and masons and the stonecutters over the control of the setting of stone. In cities where the work was in the hands of the stonecutters, the masons usually saw in the refusal of the stonecutters to set planed stone an opportunity to gain what they regarded as their rights. Here and there a branch was able to put pressure on the masons through the local building-trades council, but the local unions of the bricklayers and masons were not ordinarily affiliated with the building-trades councils. In places where the masons had jurisdiction over stone setting, it was rarely that they could be induced to refuse to set stone merely because it had been shipped in against the rule of the stonecutters.

The expectation that local contractors could aid in keeping out planer-cut stone was quickly shown to be delusive. A contractor no longer required a local stoneyard and equipment, since he could have the stone planed and cut at the quarries. The field of competition was thus greatly widened. Contracting firms with equipment at the quarry now took contracts over a large territory. The local contractors in some places undoubtedly would have been glad to see all the stonework of the locality done in their yards and by hand, but they realized that this form of local protection was impracticable.

A pronounced difference of opinion between the branches at the shipping- and the receiving-points as to the propriety of restricting the shipment of planer-cut stone soon became evident. In spirited protests the branches at Albion and Gouverneur, important shipping-points, declared that any attempt to stop the use of machinery was futile, and that they had a right to cut stone no matter where it was to be used, provided they received the same wages and worked the same number of hours. The executive board of the General Union refused for some years to grant a charter to the unaffiliated Bedford union, on the ground that the union did not coöperate in preventing the shipment of planer-cut stone into places where there were no planers.

The difficulties in the enforcement of the rule and the growing bitterness of feeling between the receiving and the shipping branches led the president of the General Union to call a national convention to meet on December 5, 1902, to consider the planer question. The advocates of restriction were greatly in the majority, and a new rule with reference to the shipment of stone was adopted. It read as follows: "This association will not countenance the transportation of cut stone from one place to another where the interchange of work is not mutually agreeable." [1]

This rule gave the branches complete local autonomy in the regulation of shipments. Even branches in which planers were in operation might now shut out planer-cut stone, merely because they wished to retain the work for their own members. Despite the strenuous opposition of the shipping branches, the rule was ratified by the branches by a vote of 145 to 103.

Under the new rule a considerable number of branches asked permission from the General Union to extend their jurisdiction over adjacent territory, in order to secure a wider monopoly for local hand-cut stone. The Louisville and New Albany branches became involved in a squabble as to which had jurisdiction over Jeffersonville, Indiana. There were planers in Louisville, but none in New Albany. The Evansville branch asked jurisdiction over Henderson, Kentucky, in order to shut

1. Constitution, 1903, Art. XII, section 1.

out planer-cut stone from Louisville. Altho the shipment of stone was not effectively checked, the branches were constantly involved in difficulties with each other over the shipments. The New Haven branch, for instance, attempted to fine members of the Springfield branch who were cutting stone for use in New Haven.

The dissatisfaction of the shipping branches constantly increased. In June, 1904, a vote on the question of excluding cut stone was demanded by a number of branches and it was finally decided to hold another convention at St. Louis in September, 1904. After much discussion and a bitter exchange of views between the representatives of the shipping branches and of the non-planer branches, the rule was remodeled by a vote of 129 to 84 to read as follows:

> This association will not countenance the transportation of cut stone from one place to another where the interchange of work is not mutually agreeable, except from branches where planers are operated by stonecutters and where wages and hours are equal at the time the contract was let. But in no case shall planer-cut stone be shipped into the jurisdiction of any branch that has succeeded in keeping the planers out of their jurisdiction.[2]

The new rule was substantially similar to the rule as it had stood prior to 1902, in that it permitted shipment into towns where planers were in operation and prohibited shipment into towns where there were no planers. The only important difference was in requiring as a condition of shipment the employment of stonecutters as planermen. The rule of 1904 was no more effective than the older rules had been, and in desperation the non-planer branches resorted to a new means of enforcement — the fining of contractors who shipped in cut stone. In October, 1905, the Memphis branch, for instance, fined a Cincinnati contractor $500 for bringing planer-cut stone into Memphis. The execu-

2. Constitution, 1905, Art. XII, section 4.

tive board of the General Union decided after much hesitation that one branch could not enforce its embargo by fining contractors whose yards were in the jurisdiction of another branch. By this time the executive board and the president of the General Union were convinced that attempts to stop the shipment of planer-cut stone were futile. The rank and file, however, were still in favor of restriction. Another convention of the General Union was held in 1906 and the shipment of planer-cut stone was much discussed, but the rule, altho changes were made in its wording, remained the same in substance.

By 1908 the situation had become intolerable. At a convention held in that year sentiment was strongly against continuing the restriction on the shipment of planer-cut stone. The majority of the "committee on the transportation of cut stone" recommended that the branches should be forbidden to restrict the shipment of stone, provided that wages and hours at the shipping- and the receiving-points were equal. Certain branches, however, notably St. Louis, complained bitterly that they had been able to keep out planer-cut stone and that this rule would force them to allow its introduction. Finally, the convention decided to repeal entirely the rule relating to the transportation of stone, leaving it to each branch to decide whether it would attempt to keep out planer-cut stone. After the rule of the General Union was repealed, a branch which determined on a policy of exclusion could not expect the aid of the shipping branches. The repeal of the rules relating to the shipment of cut stone was ratified by a branch vote of 957 to 521.

The original policy of the General Union toward the planer, as has been already noted, consisted of two parts:

first, restriction of the shipment of planer-cut stone, and, second, opposition to the introduction of planers in places where they were not in use. At the session of the General Union in 1900, when the first rule against the shipment of planer-cut stone was enacted, the branches were urged to "make every effort possible to prevent the introduction of planers in their jurisdiction." If the rule against the shipment of planer-cut stone could have been enforced, many branches would have struggled vigorously against the introduction of planers. But where it was impracticable to keep out planer-cut stone it was distinctly to the advantage of the branch to have the contractors install planers, since the members of the branch got what the machine left of the home work and, in many cases, of work for the outside. Under such conditions, therefore, the branches did not oppose the introduction of planers.[3]

Even where a union offered opposition, it received no aid from the General Union. The executive board interpreted the rule as advisory and not as mandatory, and refused to pay strike benefits where strikes were called against the introduction of planers. There were, however, some cities even of considerable population in which planers were not used for a long time. In St. Louis, for instance, planers were "abolished" in 1900 and were not installed until 1915. The success of the St. Louis branch was due to vigorous support by a strong building-trades council, which made it extremely difficult for contractors to use machine-cut stone. In 1905 the exhortation to branches to prevent the introduction of the planer was replaced by a rule which gave

3. It frequently happened that a branch which one year was strongly in favor of the prohibition of the shipment of planer-cut stone, a year later, after the installation of planers in its jurisdiction, became convinced that the planer was an economic necessity and that any attempt to interfere with shipment was futile.

the individual branches the power to "make their own local laws as to whether they will allow the introduction of the planer in their jurisdiction." [4]

Altho the national union at first confined its efforts to limiting the extension of the field of the planer, its policy was soon enlarged by rules relating to the operation of the planer. There were two of these rules: (1) the rule restricting the number of hours a planer might be operated; (2) the requirement that planermen should be stonecutters. A third rule — that a shop must employ a certain number of hand cutters for each planer — was also adopted by a number of branches, altho it never attained the dignity of a national rule. The first and third rules were designed, like the rule against the shipment of planer-cut stone and the rule against the introduction of planers, to check the displacement of hand cutters, and it will, therefore, be convenient to consider these two rules first.

The rule limiting the number of hours that planers might be operated, as has already been noted, was first introduced in 1898 by the Chicago union. The planermen in New York somewhat later adopted a similar rule, presumably at the suggestion of the stonecutters, and a few branches of the General Union followed the example thus set. The convention of the General Union held in 1902 determined to make this regulation general, and inserted the following rule in the constitution: "In no case shall planers be allowed to run or work more than the number of hours per day worked by stonecutters of said branch." [5] The enforcement of this rule was immediately found by most of the branches to be impracticable. In the quarry districts the stone was ordinarily planed at the quarries and cut in shops some

4. Constitution, 1905, Art. XII, section 5.
5. Constitution, 1903, Art. XII, section 8.

distance away. The stonecutters, therefore, could not bring pressure to bear on the owners of the planers. Moreover, it was doubtful whether the rule lessened to any considerable extent the amount of work done by the planers, since, as the Milwaukee branch pointed out, the effect of reducing hours was to increase the number of planers.[6] The limitation of hours increased the fixed charges of the contractor, but this increase was not sufficient to divert any considerable quantity of work from the machine to the hand workers. It was sufficient, however, to put a contractor in a city where the rule was enforced at a disadvantage as against his competitors in other places. Since each branch was eager to keep down the cost of production of its own contractors in order that they might be able to get contracts, only the most aggressive branches attempted to enforce the rule.

In those places where the branches did make a vigorous effort to limit the hours, they found it nearly everywhere necessary to permit some relaxation of the rule. The employers objected seriously to a rule which fixed a definite and inflexible limit, since the amount of work going to the planers fluctuated greatly. They insisted, therefore, on being allowed to operate their planers with two shifts if the amount of work was sufficient. The San Francisco branch, for instance, allowed a double shift to be used. In 1905 a new rule of the General Union legitimized the use of a double shift in case of necessity.[7] In 1907 the rule was changed from its mandatory form, and branches were merely urged to estab-

6. Stone Cutters' Journal, March, 1904, p. 7. The Chicago union had not found this rule effective in reducing the amount of planer work. In a letter to the Stone Cutters' Journal, June, 1899 (p. 13), Mr. Short, secretary of that union, said: "We were out that time in [1896] thirteen weeks and won our fight, but the victory, glorious tho it was, benefited us but little, for the contractors simply put in more planers."

7. Constitution, 1905, Art. XII, section 2.

lish an eight-hour limit on the operation of planers, with a double shift in case of necessity.[8] In 1908 the rule of the General Union was repealed. The matter was thus left to the branches. In most of those branches which had adopted eight-hour rules the pressure of competition soon forced repeal. Planers were ordinarily operated nine or ten hours, with double shifts in busy times, while the stonecutters practically everywhere had an eight hour day.[9]

The rule that a specified number of stonecutters should be employed for each planer also made its first appearance, as has been noted, in 1898 in Chicago. It was provided in the Chicago agreement that four hand cutters should be employed for each planer. In New York the local union in 1901 required the employment of five hand cutters for each planerman. The ratio varied considerably from place to place, running as high as ten to one in some places and as low as three to one in others. These rules were more irritating than restricting, since the contractor ordinarily could arrange his work so as to do on the planer all of it that could be done more economically by machinery. There were times, however, when the contractor was forced by the rule to give to his hand cutters work which could have been done more cheaply on the machine.

The final part of the policy of the union with reference to the planer was the requirement that planermen should be stonecutters. As early as 1896, as has been noted above, the Chicago union required the gradual replacement of the handy-men employed on the planers

8. Constitution, 1907, Art. XII, section 2.

9. The average number of hours in the ordinary working week of 144 planermen included in the statistics of wages and hours gathered by the Bureau of Labor in 1907 was 51.69, while the 1,064 stonecutters in the same establishments worked only 45.77 hours (Bulletin of the Bureau of Labor, No. 77, p. 50).

by stonecutters. Prior to this time the machines had been manned almost without exception by unskilled laborers who had gradually been trained to be skilled operatives. Until 1902 the General Union was still hopeful that in some way planers might be got rid of, and consequently did not concern itself with the planermen. As it became evident that shipments of planer-cut stone could not be prevented and that the number of planers was increasing, the leaders of the union began to favor a rule requiring that planermen should be stonecutters. It was argued, in the first place, that it would be difficult to enforce any limitation of hours as long as the planers were manned by handy-men. Secondly, it was felt that with the encroachments of the planer it might be necessary to find new fields of employment for stonecutters. Finally, it was contended that the strength of the union would be greatly increased by complete control over all cutting of stone, whether by hand or by machine.

Influenced by these considerations, the convention of 1902 adopted the following rule: "It is the sense of this convention that planers should be operated by members of this organization, and branches are instructed to enforce this law as soon as practicable. . . ."[1] A prime difficulty in carrying out this recommendation was the impracticability of displacing the men already employed as planermen. At the convention held in 1904 the opinion was freely expressed that some provision must be made with reference to these men, but a proposed rule authorizing the executive board to organize them in separate branches of the national union was defeated. The stonecutters were reluctant to admit to membership men who were not skilled hand cutters. Finally the convention passed a

1. Constitution, 1903, Art. XII, section 3.

rule instructing branches to require the employment of members on the planers.[2] The new rule became effective on April 1, 1905, and the branches which attempted its enforcement encountered strong opposition from the employers, who were much opposed to replacing handy-men trained to the work with high-paid workmen who were without experience in the operation of the machines. The employers, moreover, feared that the union would use this new power to limit the output of their machines. The executive board of the national union advised a gradual change in places where the planers were operated by handy-men.[3] A comparatively small number of branches did succeed in enforcing the rule, but these branches for the most part were in places where the number of planers in operation was small.

At the convention held in 1906 the rule requiring the employment of stonecutters as planermen was repealed, and it was decided to admit planermen to membership and to issue them a special card. Members were forbidden to cut, fit, or set stone planed on machines not operated by members of the stonecutters' branches.[4] Very few of the branches made any attempt to move in the matter. Most of the branches were reluctant to take handy-men into membership, and the opposition of the employers continued. At the convention of 1908, when all national rules relating to the planer were struck out, it was decided to leave in the constitution the clause permitting the admission of planermen, in order that each branch might use its own discretion in the matter.

In December, 1912, the constitution was again amended to provide for the admission of "all men operating stonecutting machinery." It was proposed that

2. Stone Cutters' Journal, October, 1904, Supplement, pp. 13, 16, 17.
3. Ibid., April, 1905, pp. 8, 9.
4. Constitution, 1907, Art. XII, section 2.

the General Union should organize separate branches of planermen in those places where they were numerous. By this time all hope that the employment of stonecutters as planermen could be generally secured was lost. The only question was whether planermen should be organized in local unions directly affiliated with the American Federation of Labor, or should be connected with the General Union.[5]

It is an open question whether training as a stonecutter is valuable to a planerman. In some shops, handy-men at relatively low rates of wages were employed as planermen; in others, even where the union did not require it, stonecutters were employed on the machines and were paid stonecutters' wages. In the small shops some elasticity in the labor supply was gained by having a planerman who could also do hand cutting. The number of stonecutters employed as planermen would have been much greater if the union had not opposed the introduction of the planer and attempted to limit its output. If the union had concentrated its energies on securing the employment of stonecutters as planermen, it might, for a time, at any rate, have carried its point. The effect of such a measure in lessening the displacement of stonecutters would have been very small, however, since the ratio of planermen to stonecutters in the country as a whole in 1915 probably did not exceed 1 to 10.

In the foregoing discussion of the machine policy of the stonecutters, attention has been directed at several points to certain difficulties in the enforcement of the rules growing out of the serious opposition in interest between the shipping and the receiving branches. But

5. Stone Cutters' Journal, January, 1913, p. 16; Constitution, 1913, Art. IV.

through a considerable part of the period from 1900 to 1915 the union had to reckon also with the powerful opposition of the associated employers and with the "dual" unions of stonecutters created by them.

As noted above, the General Union had never been able to bring into affiliation all the local unions of stonecutters. When the planer question became important in 1900 there were independent unions in Chicago, New York, and Bedford, but these unions were not antagonistic to the General Union. As long as there was only one union in each city, whether independent or affiliated, the stonecutters in that city acted together. The attempt, first by certain independent local unions and later by the General Union, to restrict the use of the planer, quickly led to the establishment in a number of cities of "dual" unions of stonecutters.

The first city in which this occurred was Chicago. During the building-trades strike of 1900 the employers organized the Independent Stone Cutters' Association. After the strike the Chicago association of cut-stone contractors employed only "independents," and in their agreement with this union it was provided that there should be "no restriction of the use of machinery or tools." In 1901 the old Chicago union applied to the General Union for a charter and this was granted; the aid of the General Union was then invoked against the "independents." In 1902 the old union published in the *Stone Cutters' Journal* a list of members of the new union, and asked other branches to "scab" these stonecutters. The "independents" were subjected to heavy fines if they wished to work in cities where the branches of the General Union were in control of stonecutting. The old union also obtained the help of the Chicago Building Trades Council in preventing, as far as possible, the employment of "independents" in Chicago.

The result of the constant warfare on the "independents" was to rouse in them a spirit of hatred to the General Union — a valuable asset to the employers when they later began to establish dual unions in other places.

The formation of a dual union in New York is directly traceable to the same cause. In September, 1904, a large group of the New York stone contractors organized an association, and demanded the removal of all restrictions on the use of machinery. The union refused to grant this demand and many of the employers began to disregard the union's rules. During the strike which followed, the contractors' association organized an independent union. The employers who were not members of the association, finding that the members of the association were able to operate their machinery free of restrictions, also demanded the removal of restrictions. The old union was too weak to refuse and reluctantly acceded. It then offered to concede the demands of the contractors' association, but that organization declared its firm intention of supporting the new union. In January, 1905, the members of the old union in large part unconditionally returned to work in the association shops.

In January, 1904, the National Cut Stone Contractors' Association was formed. One of the purposes of the new organization was to protect its members against the stonecutters and particularly against restrictions on the use of machinery. In Chicago, and later in New York, its members were closely allied with the dual stonecutters' unions; but in other cities the members of the association employed stonecutters who were members of branches of the General Union. At its second session, in November, 1904, the National Association decided to offer general resistance to all restrictions on the operation of the planers and on the shipment of stone. It adopted the following resolutions, which were to be posted in all the shops of its members: "First, that we shall run our machinery without restrictions as to hours or as to whom we shall employ to operate them; second, we shall cut and ship cut stone without any restrictions as to the place or local conditions." The adoption of these rules did not provoke a general conflict, chiefly because at the time the membership of the association was small. As it extended its influence, however, a series of engagements between the General Union and the association occurred.

As an aid in fighting the General Union, the association inspired the formation of a dual national union of stonecutters. In May, 1905, delegates from dual local unions of Pittsburgh, Chicago, and New York, together with delegates from Brooklyn, Newark, South Dover, Louisville, and Cincinnati, in which places independent unions were being formed, met in Pittsburgh and organized the National Stone Cutters' Society. The establishment of a rival national union which accepted the principle that there should be no restrictions on the use of machinery gave the employers an important advantage in combating the attempts which the General Union was making to bring about the amalgamation of the dual local unions with the branches. The local federations of labor and the building-trades councils were assisting the General Union in these efforts. Against this combination of forces the aid of a rival national union was important, since the officers of the new national union could carry on the opposition to the General Union much more effectively than the employers. It was the duty of these officers to be constantly on the alert to prevent the disintegration of the independent unions and to organize new local unions wherever the branches of the General Union refused to submit to the two rules of the National Association.

In May, 1906, one of the contractors at Toronto refused to operate his newly installed planer according to the rules of the General Union. A strike resulted, and a number of members of the National Society from the New York branch took the places of the men on strike and a branch of the National Society was formed. Branches of the National Society were organized in the same year in Washington, D.C., Bedford, Ind., and Carthage, Mo. In 1907 a branch was organized in Milwaukee. The same method was pursued in all these cases. Members of an existing branch of the National Society were sent to the city selected and after a lockout the members of the old branch were obliged to become National Society men or go to some other city for work. Here and there the branches of the old union were able after a time to bring about the amalgamation of the new union, but usually the contractors refused to deal with the amalgamated union and the branch of the society was reëstablished. Even where the amalgamation was permanent, the branch practically always was forced to give up all restrictions on the operation of the planer and on the shipment of cut stone.

After the repeal, in 1908, of the rules of the General Union relating to the planer and the shipment of cut stone, the efforts to bring about the amalgamation of the independent unions were increased. In September, 1909, the executive board of the General Union issued a proclamation offering amnesty and free admission to all members of the National Society. The American Federation of Labor and the Building Trades Department in November, 1909, declared the National Society an outlaw. The National Cut Stone Contractors' Association, on the other hand, at its convention in September, 1909, pledged its support to the National Society, and declared that after November 1 the contractors would employ only members of the society. In many of the cities where there were branches of the National Society this action immediately checked the amalgamation movement. In Bedford, however, a strike resulted. The strikers were vigorously supported by the General Union and the contractors by the National Association and by the National Society. Workmen were brought in from places where there were branches of the society, and after a long and severe struggle the General Union acknowledged its defeat.

Despite the reverse at Bedford, the General Union continued its efforts to drive the independent unions out of existence. The most effective means of attack was to secure the aid of building-trades councils in boycotting all stone which had been cut by members of the National Society. The numerous strikes resulting from the attempts of the General Union to destroy the National Society led architects to fear that if they planned to use stone in a building its erection would be delayed by strikes. The National Cut Stone Contractors' Association felt that the continuance of the conflict would be injurious to the trade by diminishing the demand for stone. Since the restrictions on the operation of the planer and on the shipment of planer-cut stone were now entirely local and confined to a small number of places, the contractors were willing to end the long struggle if the General Union was ready definitely to agree to renounce for the future all restriction on planers. The officers of the General Union on their side were anxious to bring the costly conflict to an end. The members of the National Society were for the most part desirous of reaffiliating with the General Union, and of rehabilitating themselves as "good union men." Indeed, in some cities the hold of the National Society on its branches had grown very weak.

Under these circumstances the conclusion of an agreement was not difficult. In June, 1913, the officers of the General Union, of the National Society, and of the Contractors' Association concluded a treaty of peace. Members of the National Society were to be admitted to membership in the General Union. All questions arising in the future between members of the Contractors' Association and branches of the General Union were to be settled "without cessation of work" by "arbitration," and the General Union agreed to carry out all existing contracts between the National Society and the contractors. The General Union agreed to "waive the foremanships; all stone-working machinery; shipping of stone; penalizing of National Society cutters in any manner." [6]

The agreement was attacked from two sides. The Chicago branch, embittered by the long struggle, was unwilling to admit to membership the National Society men in that city. Moreover, through the aid of the Building Trades Council, the Chicago branch had been gaining ground, and it strongly objected to having its victory snatched away; it was distinctly desirous of "penalizing National Society cutters." The agreement was also distasteful to those branches which had been able to maintain a local embargo on the shipment of planer-cut stone or to control the operation of planers. On the other hand, the branches of the General Union at Bedford, Toronto, and Milwaukee welcomed the amalgamation of the dual unions. They had long ago conceded all control over the shipment of stone and the working of the planer, and they saw in the union of all stonecutters the end of a costly feud and the promise in

6. Stone Cutters' Journal, October, 1913, inside of cover.

the near future of a substantial betterment in working conditions.

The opposition to the agreement was so strong, however, that the executive board of the General Union was convened in August, 1913. The board was not entirely satisfied with the agreement. In the first place, they desired that it should be made clear that the phrase "stone-working machinery" did not include pneumatic hammers, which were worked by stonecutters. They wished also to save to the branches which controlled the machines the right to continue to exercise such control. There was no objection on the part of the contractors to the control by the union of the air hammer, nor was there any strong objection to the continuance of control of the planer by certain local unions — notably San Francisco and St. Louis — since the Contractors' Association had no members in those cities. The union was willing to concede the shipment of stone into any branch from any other, and the Contractors' Association was willing to agree not to admit to membership contractors who were involved in any difficulty with a local branch. On this basis a supplementary agreement was made.

III

It remains to be considered what effect the introduction of the planer had on the wages, hours, and other working conditions of the stonecutters.

Table I, compiled from the report of the Bureau of Labor on "Wages and Hours of Labor, 1890 to 1907,"[7] shows the relative rates of wages paid from 1890 to 1907 to stonecutters and to certain other classes of workmen.

7. Bulletin of the Bureau of Labor, No. 77, pp. 66, 102, 103.

TABLE I

Year	Relative wages per hour			
	Stone-cutters	Granite-cutters	Marble and stone industry	Bricklayers
1890	100.5	102.8	98.5	98.4
1895	96.2	99.5	97.0	99.5
1900	100.4	108.1	104.9	106.5
1905	117.1	116.7	119.3	132.1
1907	120.8	126.5	125.7	140.9

The Bureau has not published its calculations of wages in the marble and stone industry for the years since 1907. The only data obtainable, therefore, are the statistics of union rates of wages as given in *Bulletin No. 171* of the Bureau of Labor Statistics, from which Table II is compiled.

TABLE II

Year	Relative rates of wages per hour		
	Stonecutters	Granite-cutters	Bricklayers
1907	93	90	93
1908	93	91	93
1909	93	92	93
1910	94	93	95
1911	94	93	95
1912	94	94	96
1913	96	99	98
1914	100	100	100

It may be concluded on the basis of these data that from 1900 to 1915 the wages of stonecutters rose somewhat less than those of granite-cutters, whose trade is most nearly like that of the stonecutters, and considerably less rapidly than the wages of bricklayers, the most strongly organized of the building trades. The wages of stonecutters increased less from 1895 to 1907 than wages in the marble and stone industry taken as a whole. It is extremely doubtful, however, whether the introduction of the planer can be charged with entire responsibility for the slower increase. As we have shown above, the efforts of the union to restrict the use of the planer failed almost completely, but they resulted in evoking powerful opposition from the employers and in bringing into existence strong rival unions.

The stonecutters also made a smaller reduction from 1900 to 1915 in the number of working hours per week than the other groups, as is seen from Tables III and IV, also compiled from the bulletins of the Bureau of Labor and of the Bureau of Labor Statistics already cited.

TABLE III

Year	Relative hours of work per week		
	Stonecutters	Granite-cutters	Bricklayers
1890	103.1	100.0	103.2
1895	100.2	99.9	100.0
1900	98.5	95.2	95.6
1905	95.8	92.6	92.0
1907	95.8	91.1	91.8

The slower reduction in the hours per week was partly due to the fact that the full strength of the union could not be exerted on account of the existence of the dual unions, but chiefly to the fact that the hours of stonecutters were already relatively short. In 1907 the average number of hours per week worked by stonecutters was 45.77; by granite-cutters, 47.97; by bricklayers, 46.62.[8]

8. Bulletin of the Bureau of Labor, No. 77, p. 28.

TABLE IV

Year	Relative full-time hours of work per week		
	Stonecutters	Granite-cutters	Bricklayers
1907	100	102	103
1908	100	102	103
1909	100	102	103
1910	100	101	101
1911	100	101	101
1912	100	101	101
1913	100	100	101
1914	100	100	100

It is surprising that the wages and working hours of stonecutters were not affected more by the introduction of the planer. In the face of an enormous displacement, a rival union, and a powerful employers' association, the stonecutters were able to make advances in wages and reductions in hours only slightly less than those of the granite-cutters, a well-organized trade. The explanation is to be found in the strong spirit of unionism in the trade and the powerful aid of the allied trades-councils. Altho the stonecutters are loosely organized and frequently careless in maintaining their union affiliations, they have worked for many years under standardized conditions of employment. The maintenance of these conditions has become imperatively binding.

The stonecutters do not have a system of unemployment benefits and it is impossible to ascertain to what extent the introduction of the machine was accompanied by an increase of unemployment. The adjustment of the number of stonecutters to the diminishing needs of the trade was easier than it otherwise would have been because of the method of recruiting the trade. A very considerable part of the stonecutters had always been immigrants who came to this country after having already learned the trade. A decrease in the demand had the natural effect of lessening the inflow. There is evidence, however, that unemployment, especially from 1910 to 1915, was very severe.

Besides the part it played in displacement of workmen, the machine was responsible for place dislocations by concentrating the stonecutting industry, to a considerable extent, near the quarries. A territorial redistribution of stonecutters consequently became necessary. The mobility of the stonecutters is, however, very great, and they have been able by moving from place to place to avoid, to some extent, the unemployment which would otherwise have been involved in the changes of location of the industry. As the number of workmen who can conveniently move their place of residence is limited, however, a number of local unions attempted to retain at least a share of local work. The most important method of accomplishing this end was to secure the aid of the bricklayers in enforcing a rule that jobs of less than 6,000 cubic feet must be cut locally. The stonecutters alone could not enforce such a rule, since the stone might be shipped in already cut, but if the bricklayers could be induced to refuse to set such stone, the rule could be enforced. The relations between the stonecutters and the bricklayers were cordial after the stonecutters in 1912 relinquished the setting of stone to the bricklayers, and in some places the bricklayers gave the necessary aid. At a conference between the contractors and the stonecutters in September, 1915, the former contended that the 6,000-foot rules constituted a violation of the agreement between the two organizations, but the president of the stonecutters refused to give up these rules.

The introduction of the planer and other labor-saving

devices led everywhere to considerable changes in the character of stone contracting plants. The contractors erected substantial buildings, equipped with hoisting and other devices. The sheds were usually larger, and, therefore, freer from dust, than formerly. Also, the seasonal fluctuations in employment were reduced, because the more substantial sheds heated by steam made winter work possible. These changes were due to the necessity of investing large sums in machinery and the consequent desire to run the machines as nearly continuously as possible.

CHAPTER III

THE INTRODUCTION OF SEMI-AUTOMATIC BOTTLE MACHINERY

SUMMARY

Stages in the introduction of machinery for the manufacture of glass bottles, 65.—I. The technical character of the semi-automatic machine, 67.—II. The rate of introduction, 69.—The potential displacement involved, 69.—The actual displacement, 70.—III. The jurisdiction of the unions concerned, 72.—The opposition of the Flint Glass Workers to the introduction of the machine, 73.—The jurisdictional confliet between the Glass Bottle Blowers and the Flint Glass Workers, 76.—IV. The machine policy of the Glass Bottle Blowers, 79.—V. Effect of the machine on wages and hours of labor, 81.—Estimate of the validity of the policy of the Glass Bottle Blowers, 83.

THE art of blowing glass into the form of jars and bottles is one of the oldest of existing crafts; it antedates by centuries the art of printing from movable type and is coeval with the smelting of iron. By the original method — ordinarily known as off-hand blowing — the blower formed the bottle by alternate blowing and twirling until it assumed the desired shape. This method is still followed in making certain articles, but for ordinary bottles and jars the off-hand method has long been superseded by mold blowing.

The manufacture of bottles and jars by the method of mold blowing is carried on by working units known as "shops." In each of these there are seven persons — three skilled workmen and four boys. Two of the men blow and the third finishes. The blower takes a lump of glass from the pot or tank on his pipe, rolls and partially blows it. The mold tender, a boy, opens an iron mold and the blower lowers the glass into the mold. The mold having been closed, the blower inflates the glass to fill the mold. The pipe is cracked off from the bottle or jar, which is then carried by another boy — known as the "snapping-up boy" — to the finisher, who shapes with tools the neck and lip of the bottle. A third boy — the "carrying-in boy" — carries the ware to the annealing lehr. A "cleaning-off boy" cleans the blow pipes of the blowers in preparation for re-use. Variations in this arrangement are found. In making some kinds of bottles, for example, a gathering boy gathers the glass for the blower, but the rules of the union have severely restricted this form of the division of labor except on very heavy ware.

Since 1898 the manufacture of bottles and jars has been revolutionized by the introduction of machinery, but the change from the older hand technique has been accomplished by a series of innovations. In most other trades in which machinery has displaced handicraft, the original machine has been improved upon, but the improvements have not radically changed its character. In the manufacture of glass bottles, on the contrary, the struggle between handicraftsman and machine has been complicated by a struggle of machine against machine. The machines successively introduced for the manufacture of glass bottles differ from each other not only in their technical character, but also in the two particulars most important in any study of the introduction of machinery — the degree to which the machine displaces hand labor, and the extent to which skilled labor is required for its operation.

The history of the introduction of machinery for the manufacture of bottles consequently falls into three periods, each of which is characterized by the introduction of a new form of machine:

1. From 1898 to 1905, semi-automatic machines, requiring for their effective working skilled workmen, largely displaced hand blowers in the manufacture of wide-mouth ware.

2. From 1905 to 1917, the Owens automatic machine, which required only supervision and the amount of whose product was independent of the speed of the watcher, was the chief factor in the displacement of hand blowers and of the skilled operatives of semi-automatic machines. Contemporaneous with the introduction of the Owens was the appearance of semi-automatic machines for making narrow-mouth ware.

3. From 1917 to 1924, the trade has again been revolutionized by the introduction of "feed and flow devices" which, while requiring more attention than the Owens machine, produce more ware than the semi-automatics. The attendants, moreover, need not be skilled workers, altho the question of the relative superiority of skilled and unskilled workmen as attendants is still in dispute.

The present paper deals with only the first of these periods — the one characterized by the introduction of semi-automatic machines for manufacturing wide-mouth ware.

I

The fundamental principle in all semi-automatic machines for making bottles and jars is the combination of pressing and blowing. These two methods were first united as a means of fashioning large pieces of table ware. In 1865 Gillinder, for example, patented a method of making glass pitchers by first pressing and then blowing. The blowing, however, was not in a mold, but served merely to hold the article distended while it was shaped by tools. Also, in 1873 Atterbury patented a process by which a lump of glass was pressed to form the top of an article, the bottom of the pressing mold was then dropped, and the glass was expanded by blowing into the shape of the blowing mold. Gillinder's method was used to some extent, but apparently Atterbury's device was never used commercially. In 1881 Philip Arbogast patented a combined pressing and blowing device, in which the top of the article was first pressed; the article was then removed to a blowing mold and by means of mechanically-applied air pressure expanded to the shape of the mold. In 1884 Mr. D. C. Ripley, of Pittsburgh, a manufacturer of table ware, began to use the Arbogast machine, and in 1885 purchased the patent rights. The Arbogast method was used by Mr. Ripley in manufacturing certain kinds of table ware, and large containers such as druggists' jars.

The Arbogast machine, however, was used to a very limited extent and hardly at all on ordinary jars and bottles until 1893, when the Enterprise Glass Company secured the right to use the machine and commenced to make vaseline jars. Licenses were issued to several other manufacturers, and considerable quantities of "packers' goods" were made, that is, jars and wide-mouth bottles for liquids and pastes. Improvements were soon made on the original machines. The most important of these was the development of a combined pressing and blowing mold, by which the need for the removal of the article from the press mold was obviated. By 1896 the first of the new machines was in successful operation at the Atlas Glass Works, Washington, Pennsylvania, and in 1898 similar machines were installed by Ball Brothers, the largest manufacturer of fruit jars. Each machine required two operators. One, known as the "gatherer," gathered the glass from the tank; another, the "presser," cut off the glass and managed the lever which controlled the plunger and the air pressure. From this time, the use of the machine rapidly widened. By 1905 a great variety of wide-mouth ware — fruit jars, ink bottles, vaseline jars, milk jars—was being made on the machine.

II

It is impossible to give more than a rough estimate of the number of the machines in use by years, but the following table is approximately correct:

Number of Semi-automatic Machines in Use, 1897–1905

1897	20	1900	80	1903	150
1898	50	1901	90	1904	200
1899	60	1902	100	1905	250[1]

A measure of the amount of possible displacement of hand blowers involved in the introduction of the semi-automatic machines may be had by assuming that the relative production by hand and by machine on all wide-mouth ware was the same as that in the manufacture of fruit jars, where the facts as to the amount of displacement have been recorded.[2] Three hand blowers working as a "shop" had been able to make 3600 quart fruit jars in a day. One presser and one gatherer operating a machine could make in a day 4300 quart jars, or considerably more than three blowers. Since the machines were ordinarily operated for two shifts, we may allow a displacement of six hand blowers for each machine. As the total number of machines in operation in 1905 was 250, we have a potential displacement of hand

1. Of the total number of machines in operation in 1905, 120 were in factories controlled by the Glass Bottle Blowers' Association, 75 in factories controlled by the Flint Glass Workers' Union, and the remainder in nonunion plants.

2. This assumption underestimates somewhat the capacity of the machines in terms of hand labor, since fruit jars were not finished by skilled blowers, but by handy-men. On other ware, such as milk jars, where one of the three men in the shop worked as finisher, the displacement due to the machine was greater than on fruit jars.

blowers of about 1500. That is, in 1905 an amount of work was being done on the machines which, if done by hand, would have required the work of 1500 hand blowers. Since the number of glass-bottle blowers in the United States in 1897 was probably not more than 6000, one fourth of them would have been thrown out of work if the potential displacement had been realized.

As a matter of fact, almost no displacement occurred. This result was due chiefly to the great increase in the production of glass jars and bottles during the period under discussion. The following table, taken from the Census of Manufactures, shows by classes the number of bottles produced in the years 1899 and 1904:

PRODUCTION OF BOTTLES AND JARS, 1899 AND 1904

(*In gross*)

	1899	1904	Per cent of increase
Prescriptions, vials, and druggists' wares	2,423,932	3,202,586	32
Beer, soda, and mineral	1,351,118	2,351,852	73
Liquors and flasks	985,374	2,157,801	119
Milk jars	146,142	253,651	73
Fruit jars	789,298	1,061,289	34
Patent and proprietary	1,296,131	1,657,372	29
Packers and preservers	784,588	1,237,065	57

The greater part of this increase — amounting in the aggregate to nearly 50 per cent — was entirely independent of the introduction of the machine. Of the seven classes of ware enumerated, the machine was used only on milk jars, fruit jars, and packers' goods. The increase in the production of these classes of goods was far less than sufficient to offset the displacement due to the machine, even if all the men employed on the machines had been former hand blowers. The demand for bottles was not stimulated by the lower price sufficiently to compensate for the economy in labor. The elasticity of demand for glass bottles appears to be very small.

The cost of the glass container for most products is only a small part of the total cost, and a reduction in the price of the container therefore stimulates very little the demand for the article. Also, the extent to which glass is substituted as a container for tin or paper appears to be dependent more on slow changes in taste than on cost. During the period under discussion there was some extension in the use of wide-mouth bottles as containers. Candies, meats, and tobacco, for example, in 1905 were being sold in glass packages. The superiority of the machine-made product in finish and in uniformity of content also increased somewhat the sale of containers.[3] But in the main the great extension in the use of bottles and jars from 1899 to 1904 was due either to an increase in the consumption of the article, in no way affected by a change in the price of the container, as was the case with beer bottles, or to changes in taste which demanded glass-packed goods for sanitary reasons.

The potential displacement of hand blowers from the trade was met in two ways: (1) by the conversion of jar blowers into blowers of other forms of ware unaffected by the machine, (2) by placing hand blowers in positions as machine workers. The first of these methods was practicable because of the great increase in the production of glass bottles. From 1897 to 1905, the number of hand bottle blowers in the United States increased from six thousand to nine thousand. Unfortunately, there were some classes of blowers so highly specialized that it was impossible to convert them. Many blowers of fruit jars, for example, could not readily become blowers of beer bottles.[4] Moreover, where the factory was devoted

3. In 1897, the prices for machine-made fruit jars was higher than that for hand-made jars. Proceedings, Glass Bottle Blowers' Association, 1898, p. 56.

4. Testimony of D. A. Hayes, in Report of Industrial Commission, vol. vii, p. 111.

entirely to the production of a single line of ware, and that line of ware was taken over by the machine, it was necessary for a workman to move to some other factory if he was to continue as a hand blower.

The second method of avoiding displacement — the conversion of hand blowers into machine workers — was far less important as a device for reducing displacement from the trade. This was due partly to the disinclination of blowers to take places on the machine, partly to the reluctance of the employers to employ hand blowers as machine workers, but chiefly to an unfortunate struggle between the two unions in the trade.

III

Until 1913 the jurisdiction over the jar and bottle trade was divided between two unions, the Flint Glass Workers and the Glass Bottle Blowers. The original line of demarcation between the unions was based on the difference in the kind of glass used. The Flint Glass Workers worked with flint glass, made in covered pots, while the Green Glass Workers — as the present union of Glass Bottle Blowers was known for many years — used green glass, made in open pots. The price for making articles from open pots was less than the price charged for making articles from covered pots. Consequently, most kinds of jars and bottles were made from green glass. Only the higher grades of bottles, such as prescription bottles, were made from flint glass. Moreover, in making articles by pressing, flint glass was almost always used. The result was that the Green Glass Workers were confined to blowing bottles and jars, while the Flint Glass Workers had branches of pressers as well as of blowers.

With the introduction of the tank, in the nineties, the line of division between the trades becomes blurred, since flint glass of good quality can be made in the tank. As the list price of the Green Glass Workers was lower than that of the Flints for similar articles, the bottles formerly made by the Flints rapidly came to be made in factories controlled by the Green Glass Workers. In 1895, this change was signalized by a change in the name of the United Green Glass Workers' Association to the Glass Bottle Blowers' Association. In 1900, the prescription branch of the Flints — blowers of prescription bottles — against the wishes of that organization, went over bodily to the Glass Bottle Blowers. At the time the machine was introduced, therefore, the relations between the Flints and the Bottle Blowers were already much strained.

The machine was first used, as has already been noted, in making flint glass ware, such as table ware and globe jars. Its use in making small packers' jars was begun experimentally in 1891, but was discontinued because the Flint Glass Workers, who controlled the Ripley factory, insisted that the "move" — the amount which might be made by a workman in a half-day — should be fixed.[5] At that time, there was no move in the prescription department, but there was in the pressed-ware department. Since the articles in question were partly made by pressing, the president of the Flints held that the number to be made must be limited, and that the limit was to be in accordance with the amount or-

5. In his testimony in the case of the United States Glass Company *vs.* Atlas Glass Company, Mr. Ripley said, "The policy of the labor organization has been that no device that lessened the amount of skill would be operated except for the same amount of money as was paid for the full exercise of skill in the manufacture of the article by new processes. Also any new device which enabled the workmen to make more with less labor could not be used to advantage from the fact that the numbers were limited to the number determined by the labor organization." (Defendant's Brief in United States Glass Company *vs.* Atlas Glass Company, p. 85.)

dinarily made in the prescription branch of similar articles by blowing.[6] The net result of this ruling was that the machine labor cost was to be identical with the cost of hand manufacture.

Mr. Ripley then ceased the manufacture of machine-made jars in his own factory and licensed a number of other manufacturers to use the machine on packers' goods. The factories which thus began work with the machine were all nonunion.[7] In 1895, the president of the Flints called attention to the increasing use of the machine, and discussed the proper policy of the union. He was now convinced that the machine should be worked by the members of the union. "By working it and finding it successful," he said, "we could minimize its dangers by buying from the owner . . . or we could so arrange the prices for working it as to leave it little or no advantage and thus avoid placing our association in the position of opposing useful machinery." [8]

In 1896, one of the largest union glass factories in the country requested the Flints to make a wage-list for pressed-and-blown bottles, and asserted that the class of work made on the machine was being rapidly taken from

6. Proceedings, Flint Glass Workers' Union, 1893, p. 19. President Smith said: "Within the past few months a dark cloud has arisen in the horizon of the Prescription Department. We refer to the machine for making bottles by the dual process of pressing and blowing. The machine was brought to our notice by reason of a dispute over the number that should constitute a move of the 2 oz. and wages therefor. It appears that a shop made about 900 for one half-day's work. The firm demanded 1200. We advised a move on the basis of the Prescription List. This, of course, was not satisfactory to Mr. Ripley. Under favorable conditions it is no exaggeration to say that a shop can produce four thousand 2 oz. bottles in a day's work." At the same convention, Vice-President Hinckley said: "What we want is to put the cost of production equal on the machine- and hand-made article." (Ibid., p. 48.)

7. In his testimony in the case of the United States Glass Company *vs.* the Atlas Glass Company, Mr. Ripley said, "In all cases where we have granted licenses it has been necessary that the parties operating the device first rid themselves of the domination of the union."

8. Proceedings, Flint Glass Workers, 1895, p. 61.

union houses, partly on account of the superiority of the machine product. A price-list for machine-made bottles, accordingly, was approved by the convention.[9] Apparently, however, very few union gatherers or pressers were employed on the machines until they were introduced into the factory of Ball Brothers. This firm was employing at the time several hundred members of the Glass Bottle Blowers' Union and the machine was intended to take over at once a part of, and ultimately all, the work of these hand blowers.

When the machines were started at Ball Brothers factory, the Blowers had no policy with reference to the introduction of machinery. It is true there was a rule dating from 1892 among the by-laws of the association, which prohibited any member from "using Ashley's bottle-blowing machine or any other bottle-blowing machine"; but this was not seriously regarded. The convention of 1898, after discussing the introduction of the machine in the fruit-jar houses, had decided to leave the matter in the hands of the president and executive board "to make the best settlement and upon the most advantageous terms that they can get."[1] The president and executive board, so far from refusing permission to members to operate machines, urged insistently that the displaced blowers should be employed on the machines. Ball Brothers were reluctant to accede to this request. In the first place, they wished to put skilled pressers on the machines; in the second place, they distrusted the good will of the displaced blowers toward the machine. Moved by these considerations

9. Proceedings, Flint Glass Workers, 1896, pp. 145, 203, 240. The rates for gatherers in press houses were to be from $1.47 to $1.54 per turn. In prescription houses 8-oz. bottles were to be made at the rate of 28¼ cents per gross, of which 16½ cents was to go to the presser and 11¾ cents to the gatherer.

1. Proceedings, Glass Bottle Blowers, 1898, p. 75.

they manned their first machines with pressers who were members of the Flint Glass Workers' Union.[2] Later in the year, however, they gave places on additional machines to members of the association. For a considerable period some of their tanks were worked by Flints and some by Blowers.

From 1898 to 1913, when a jurisdictional agreement between the Bottle Blowers and the Flints was concluded, the two unions were engaged in a constant struggle over control of the machines. The Flints contended that the work belonged to them, since they had jurisdiction over pressing. The Bottle Blowers on their side maintained that jurisdiction belonged to them, since the machines made bottles and displaced bottle blowers.

Two things favored the Blowers. In the first place, it was obvious that if blowers could be taught to do the required work, a considerable amount of displacement might be obviated. The Blowers, therefore, were under strong inducement to secure control of the machines. Secondly, since the machines were in most cases introduced in bottle houses and since the kinds of bottles they could make were limited, the employers were reluctant to break with the association and perhaps lose their force of hand blowers. The Blowers finally succeeded in establishing their jurisdiction over the machines, but the conflict of the two unions was not conducive to strength in dealing with the machine question and employers not infrequently extorted concessions by pitting one union against the other.

At first an arrangement was made that a member of one union working in a factory under the jurisdiction of the other union should retain his membership in his own union, but pay the trade assessment of the union under whose jurisdiction he was working. In 1900, the Blowers

2. Proceedings, Glass Bottle Blowers, 1898, p. 12.

proposed that Flints working in association factories should become members of the association, and *vice versa*, but the Flints refused to accept the proposal. In his annual report for 1901 the president of the Flints declared that this proposal was designed to secure the control of the machines to the Blowers, and contended that the Blowers could not furnish competent gatherers and pressers from their own members, and wished to use the Flint workmen to satisfy employers until the Blowers could train gatherers and pressers from their own number.[3] The Flint convention of 1901 accordingly forbade its members who were working on machines to pay assessments to the Blowers. At Olean, New York, in March, 1902, when the Flint gatherers and pressers refused to pay, they were replaced by workmen taken, as alleged by the Flints, from nonunion plants.[4] In 1902, the convention of the Blowers definitely decided that all machines in association factories should be operated by members of the Blowers' union.[5]

The Flints made reprisals wherever possible. The difficulty which they faced, however, was that the Blowers controlled the supply of skilled hand blowers and the Flints could not furnish the required blowers to the bottle houses. It was evident that, unless some method could be devised for securing blowers, the association would entirely control the machines. The work of a bottle machine presser differs somewhat from that of the presser in ordinary press houses, and the manufacturers who were installing machines naturally turned to the union with which they were already in relations and which controlled the majority of machine pressers.

Under these circumstances the Flints cast about for

3. Proceedings, Flint Glass Workers, 1901, p. 60.
4. Ibid., 1902, pp. 55, 56.
5. Proceedings, Glass Bottle Blowers, 1902, p. 110.

some means of getting blowers. By a remarkable coincidence they found a source ready to hand. For many years, the prescription department of the Flints had suffered severely from the competition of nonunion houses making whiskey flasks. In 1899, the union decided that it would be cheaper to erect a factory and make flasks even at a very low price than it would be to attempt to force the flask houses into the union by strikes. The union hoped that when the nonunion houses found that the price was unprofitable they would unionize their plants. Accordingly, a factory was equipped for making flasks at Summitville, Indiana. After the prescription department went over to the association, in 1900, the Flints no longer had any incentive to use the plant for its original purpose. It was decided to continue the operation of the plant with the purpose of training up blowers to supply manufacturers who were willing to use Flint semi-automatic machine workers. In 1903, the president of the Flints said, "We have demonstrated our ability to make bottle blowers, and should make them in Summitville as fast as it is necessary to use them to protect our members from being compelled to join the Greens or lose their job. The Summitville factory is our powerful weapon of defence." [6] In June, 1903, in a controversy with the association over a machine factory, the president of the Flints offered to supply the manager with bottle blowers if the association struck the plant on account of the refusal of the Flint machine pressers to pay dues to the association.[7] A few days later the Summitville factory was burned and a plan for the erection of a new factory was rejected by the union.[8]

6. Proceedings, Flint Glass Workers, 1903, p. 146; Journal Flint Glass Workers, November, 1912, p. 211; National Glass Budget, July 11, 1903.
7. Proceedings, Flint Glass Workers, 1903, p. 139.
8. Ibid., pp. 286, 296.

The Blowers retaliated by invading branches of work belonging to the Flints. In 1904, they secured jurisdiction over the plant of the Illinois Glass Company at Alton, Illinois, and took into membership not only seventy-five Flint machine workers, but a certain number of iron-mold workers and caster-place workers, branches of the glass trade over which the Flints had jurisdiction.[9] The constant warfare greatly impeded both the Blowers and the Flints in attempts to improve the working conditions of the machine workers. By 1905, however, the issue was fairly well decided in favor of the Blowers.

IV

The Blowers' policy with reference to the new machines was confined at the outset entirely to securing control of the machine in order to make it possible to transfer hand blowers to machine work. Even so, the outlook was discouraging. The machines had been worked hitherto almost exclusively in nonunion plants. The work on the machine was admittedly of a kind for which hand blowers would need a period of training. The union hoped that the general knowledge of the glass trade possessed by the hand blowers would enable them expeditiously to master the technique of the machine, but employers were inclined to be skeptical. To force the employment of displaced hand blowers on the machine, the union had only one weapon against employers — the threat to withdraw their hand blowers. But as things stood in 1898 the union could not afford to place much reliance on this resource of enforcement, as there were too many blowers beyond the control of the association. The prescription department of the Flints had not been absorbed, and nonunion glass-bottle blowers

9. Proceedings, Flint Glass Workers, 1905, pp. 74, 76.

were numerous. At a conference with Ball Brothers in February, 1897, President Hayes "informed them that the association would not interfere with them in the introduction of jar-making machinery but would expect them to employ union labor and also request them to give our men the preference; provided, of course, they proved themselves capable of operating the machines after gaining some knowledge of them." [1] The Blowers in 1898, however, as has been noted, allowed the firm to man its new machines with Flint pressers and gatherers, contenting itself with the promise that the firm would later employ Blowers on part of its machines. In September, 1898, some ninety members of the Blowers' union went to work on the machines.

The rules adopted for recruiting machine workmen were not well suited, on their face, to securing the conversion of blowers into machine operators. The work of operating the machines was recognized as a separate department in the trade, with its own rules. The learner in the machine department began as a gatherer. For one year, he worked at 10 per cent less than the journeyman gatherer's wage. At the end of the year he became a member of the association and a journeyman gatherer. A journeyman gatherer had to work three years before he was entitled to press, and meanwhile his wage was 75 per cent of that of a presser. If these rules had been strictly enforced against hand blowers, the process or conversion obviously would have been a rigorous one — equivalent indeed to learning a new trade. But the rules were not applied against journeymen hand blowers, who were allowed to become full-fledged gatherers, or even pressers, whenever employers were willing to hire them. In an expanding trade it would have been quite possible for numbers of hand blowers to become

1. Proceedings, Glass Bottle Blowers, 1897, p. 34.

pressers. As a matter of fact comparatively few in this period made the step. The blowers of wide-mouth ware preferred for the most part to go over to other branches of the trade, where work was abundant. Indeed, the problem of furnishing workmen to man the new machines was often perplexing to the officers of the union.

One other policy was strongly urged on the union — the reduction of the hand list for ware manufactured on the machine also. In 1896, the manufacturers asked, at the annual wage conference, that the hand price for fruit jars be reduced 25 per cent as a means of meeting machine competition. The Blowers refused. In 1898, after the machines had been widely introduced in fruit-jar factories, the officers of the union agreed to reduce the price for making ordinary fruit jars by hand 45 per cent. This was done, however, only after one of the leading manufacturers of fruit jars had started one of his plants with nonunion men.[2] Despite the reduction, machines were introduced the next year in the plant of this manufacturer. After this experience the union steadily refused, during the period under discussion, to reduce the hand list on other ware in order to meet the competition of machine ware.

V

There remains to be considered the effect of the narrow-mouth semi-automatic, on the wages, hours, and other working conditions of the workers. Unfortunately, no exact statistical material is available, since the Bureau of Labor Statistics has not included bottle blowing among the industries covered by its wage studies. Since the Bottle Blowers are piece-workers, readjustment of working conditions frequently affects earnings

2. Proceedings, Glass Bottle Blowers, 1899, p. 12.

as much as changes in the piece rates, and these readjustments are not recorded.[3]

In 1898, when the semi-automatic was introduced, the hand blowers were working at a discount of 15 per cent from their standard hand list. By two increases made in 1899 and 1900 they again reached the level of the net list, and maintained this scale during the period under consideration. The standard working day for hand blowers at the time of the introduction of the semi-automatic machine was eight and one-half hours' actual working time. Glass factories for the most part worked two shifts and the men on the night shift alternated weekly with the men on the day shift. The week's work terminated at 3 A.M. on Sunday morning, and began again on Monday at 7 A.M. In 1898, the union secured from the manufacturers the abolition of the Saturday night shift, thus reducing the working week to eleven shifts. In 1903, the union tried to secure the cessation of work at twelve o'clock on Saturdays, and was able to obtain an agreement to stop at four o'clock, a net reduction of forty-five minutes in the weekly hours of work.[4] In general, it may be safely said that neither the standard rate nor the length of the working day of hand blowers was adversely affected by the introduction of the semi-automatic. So rapidly was the demand for glass bottles increasing that throughout the period a constant scarcity of hand blowers manifested itself.

Much less favorable were the conditions of those hand blowers who, from one cause or another, were forced to

3. In 1900, when the restoration of the net list was under consideration, the employers submitted detailed wage statistics which showed that the average daily earnings of the blowers in 1899–1900 at the reduced list price were $5.46, while in the year 1894, before prices for blowing were reduced, the average was $4.94. (Proceedings, Glass Bottle Blowers, 1900, pp. 48, 49.)

4. Minutes of the Final Conference, 1903, p. 24. The hour of quitting was made four o'clock instead of five, but the workers conceded the afternoon "tempo" or pause of fifteen minutes.

become machine operators. The machine piece rate for fruit jars — the basic rate for all semi-automatic machine rates — established in 1898, was the rate then being paid in nonunion machine plants.[5] This rate was accepted by the Flints and later by the Blowers. Doubtless, if the situation had been different, a higher rate might have been obtained. The rivalry between the unions and the existence of a large body of nonunion machine workers precluded any effective action for a higher rate. At the outset the earnings of blowers who went on the machines was probably not more than half their old earnings. But the output increased rapidly with improvements in the machines and with the increasing adaptation of the men to the machines. The piece rate was increased in 1903, and by 1905 the average wage of skilled machine men was as high as the average for hand blowers. The nine-hour day originally agreed upon in 1898 remained in force in 1905.

That the union was not affected adversely by the introduction of the semi-automatic machine is clearly indicated by the increasing control exercised over the trade. In 1896, Mr. Denis Hayes, then vice-president of the union, in charge of the organization of nonunionists, made a careful census of union and nonunion bottle blowers. He found in all 6229 bottle blowers, of whom 4200 were in the unions and 2029 were nonunionists. In 1907, a similar census was taken with the result that of 10,997 skilled workers, including machine operators, 9627 were found to be in the union. The menace of nonunion competition, which in 1897 had been the chief concern of the Bottle Blowers, had almost ceased to exist by 1907.

The virtue of the Blowers' policy was not so much that it reduced the displacement caused by the wide-

5. Proceedings, Glass Bottle Blowers, 1898, p. 11.

mouth semi-automatic machine — altho even in this respect something was gained — as that it established a rule under which future displacement might be avoided. It was reasonable to anticipate in 1898 that future machine development would take the line of a gradual adaptation of semi-automatic machines to other lines of ware. By 1905, the Blowers had placed themselves in a position to cope with such a development. Unfortunately for the union, while the anticipated extension of the range of semi-automatic machinery did occur, the whole problem was complicated by the introduction of automatic machines. But even so, the policy of the union in establishing its control over semi-automatic machinery bore fruit in the form of some reduction in the amount of displacement.

CHAPTER IV

THE INTRODUCTION OF AUTOMATIC BOTTLE MACHINES

SUMMARY

UNTIL 1905 the only important change from primitive hand methods in the manufacture of glass bottles and jars was the introduction of semi-automatic machines for making wide-mouth bottles. From 1905 to the present time, the proportion of the total production of bottles and jars made on automatic machines has constantly increased. In 1917 it was 50 per cent; in 1922–23, 80 per cent;[1] and in 1924–25, 90 per cent. Corresponding changes have occurred in the character of the labor force. In 1905, when the automatic machine was still unimportant as a factor in production, the production of the 12,000,000 gross of bottles made in the United States required 10,000 skilled workmen and apprentices, of whom 9000 were hand blowers and 1000 were operators of semi-automatic machines.[2] In 1924 the production of 18,000,000 gross of bottles[3] was

1. Manufacturers' Report of Final Wage Conference, 1923, p. 7.
2. Proceedings, Glass Bottle Blowers, 1907, p. 43.
3. Unfortunately, the Bureau of the Census in 1921 and 1923 did not collect data as to the quantity of bottles manufactured. The Census of Manufactures, 1919, is the last, therefore, in which this information is given. The Glass Container Association has courteously furnished the

achieved by approximately 1000 hand blowers, 300 operators of semi-automatic machines, and 1500 attendants of automatic machines. The decrease in skilled and semi-skilled workers from 10,000 in 1905 to less than 3000 in 1924 by no means completely measures the reduction in the amount of labor required. Of the 8000 or more unskilled helpers, mostly boys, who aided in the hand and semi-automatic manufacture, nine-tenths have been made unnecessary.

The introduction of automatic machinery in the glass-bottle industry falls into two periods.

A. From 1905 to 1917, the Owens machine, the only important form of automatic machine in use, was rapidly introduced. This period was marked also by a great extension in the use of semi-automatic machines, especially of those for the manufacture of narrow-mouth ware.

B. The period from 1917 to the present has been characterized by the introduction of flow and feed devices, also automatic in character. The flow and feed devices have displaced chiefly the operators of semi-automatic machines, but they have also had some effect in displacing hand workmen. The two periods will be dealt with separately.

(A) The Introduction of the Owens Bottle Machine

The Owens machine was the logical extension of the semi-automatic bottle machine, which, in its latest forms, requires hand labor only in getting the glass from the furnace to the machine in proper quantities. The

writer with data as to the production of bottles in 1920–22 inclusive. On the basis of these figures, with allowance for the normal increase in the use of bottles and for change in the rate of business activity, the estimate of 18,000,000 gross in 1924 has been made.

Owens machine, by suction, draws the glass in the required amount from the tank, thus making the entire process automatic.[4] The saving in labor cost on the Owens machine over other methods in use at the time of its introduction was large. In 1906, the Owens Company stated that the labor cost of manufacturing a gross of pint beer bottles by the Owens machine was 10 cents against $1.47 by hand. The labor cost of manufacturing a gross of pint milk bottles was 10 cents against 75 cents on the semi-automatic. Moreover, the Owens machine was soon improved. The carrying-in boys were displaced by automatic leers, and the daily output of the later models was much increased. These improvements widened the difference in labor cost between the Owens machine and alternative methods of manufacture. In quality of product, also, the Owens machine was superior, in that the bottles made by it were far more nearly uniform in weight and content than those made by hand or on the semi-automatic machines. Uniformity of content has become extremely important in recent years, partly through the increasing stringency of the laws relating to measures, and partly through the greater use of filling machines.

I

The following table shows the number of Owens machines in operation in the United States from 1905 to 1917:[5]

4. The inventor of the Owens machine, Mr. M. J. Owens, a bottle blower by trade, made many other important inventions — notably the tumbler machine and the lamp-chimney machine. From 1895 to his death in 1923 he was constantly engaged in experimentation. It may fairly be said that his contributions to the mechanics of glass manufacture have been unequalled in importance in the history of the industry.

5. The figures are taken from the annual reports of the Glass Bottle Blowers' Association.

NUMBER OF OWENS MACHINES IN OPERATION IN THE UNITED STATES — 1905–17

1905–1906	8	1911–1912	124
1906–1907	18	1912–1913	152
1907–1908	34	1913–1914	164
1908–1909	46	1914–1915	176
1909–1910	61	1915–1916	187
1910–1911	103	1916–1917	200

In estimating the potential displacement of bottle blowers involved in the introduction of the Owens machine, the increase in the productivity of the machine is a factor of prime importance. The daily output of pint beer bottles may be taken as an index of this increase. The original contracts for the use of the machine were based on an estimated output of 100 gross in twenty-four hours. The machine actually produced 125 gross. In 1909 a new style of machine, the 10-arm, was introduced with a capacity of 200 gross. The new type, however, only gradually replaced the older. In 1914 other improvements were made in the machine, with the result that in 1917 the average run on the newest type of machine was 350 gross of pint beers. When allowance is made for these changes, it may be estimated that the annual capacity of all the Owens machines in operation in gross of bottles increased as follows:

1909	1,500,000	1912	7,000,000
1910	2,500,000	1913	8,000,000
1911	4,200,000	1914	11,000,000

The amount of potential displacement may be calculated in another way. It has been reckoned by a competent authority that one Owens machine in 1917 was capable of producing as much as 54 hand blowers.[6] The 200 machines operating in 1917, therefore, were

6. The Glass Industry as affected by the War: Tariff Information Series No. 5, p. 139.

equal in capacity to 10,000 hand blowers. In 1917, therefore, the Owens machines in operation were capable of producing almost as many bottles as the total production amounted to in 1905, or, put in another way, something more than the 9000 hand blowers at work in 1905.

In the meantime, however, as the following table shows, the production of bottles had increased very rapidly.

PRODUCTION OF BOTTLES AND JARS, 1904, 1909, 1914, 1919
(In thousands of gross)

	1904	1909	1914	1919
Prescriptions	3,202	3,624	4,893	6,684
Beer, soda, and mineral	2,351	2,345	4,573	4,178
Liquors and flasks	2,157	1,887	2,689	993
Milk jars	253	440	1,188	877
Fruit jars	1,061	1,124	1,198	1,860
Battery jars	19	9	79	13
Patent and proprietary	1,657	1,637	1,384	3,364
Packers' and preservers'	1,237	1,237	3,271	4,297
Demijohns and carboys	5	10	13	23
Total	11,942	12,313	19,288	22,289

If the production of bottles and jars in 1917 is estimated at 24,000,000 gross,[7] it may be inferred from the preceding calculations of the capacity of the Owens machine that nearly one half of the 1917 production was on Owens machines.[8] The other half was made by hand and on semi-automatic machines. The number of glass bottles produced in 1917 by hand blowers and the

7. The year 1917 was a peculiarly prosperous year in the glass-bottle industry. The fall in production in 1919 was due largely to the fact that the Eighteenth Amendment became effective in January, 1920, and, the breweries and distilleries were not replenishing their stocks of bottles.

8. This estimate agrees approximately with the statement of Mr. T. W. Rowe, Statistician of the Owens Bottle Company, to the United States Tariff Commission in 1918. Mr. Rowe put the production on the Owens machine at 45 per cent of the total. Tariff Information Series No. 5, Washington, 1918, p. 129.

operators of semi-automatic machines, taken together, was therefore approximately equal to the amount produced in 1905 by the same classes of workers. But the proportion of hand blowers to machine operators changed greatly from 1905 to 1917. While in 1905, as has been noted, the hand blowers numbered 9000 and the operators 1000, in 1917 the hand blowers numbered 2000 and the operators 2000.

II

In view of the great superiority of the Owens machine both in labor cost and in quality of product, it appears surprising at first sight that any work was left to the hand blowers or to the operators of semi-automatic machines. The factors responsible for so large a survival of the older technique may be grouped under four heads: (1) the policy adopted by the owners of the Owens patents in marketing the invention, (2) the nature of the demand for bottles, (3) the development of the semi-automatic machine, and (4) the time required for the adaptation of the Owens machine to the manufacture of the various classes of bottles.

(1) Three methods of marketing the machine were open to the owners of the Owens patents: they might sell or lease the machine to any one who was willing to pay the price or royalty, grant licenses to selected manufacturers, or themselves manufacture bottles. The Company has followed both the second and third methods. Until about 1914, however, the greater part of the production on Owens machines was in the factories of licensees. The manufacturers who secured licenses specialized in particular lines of ware.[9] The manufacture of any one line of ware on Owens machines was, therefore, carried on in only a few factories. It

9. The Glass Industry, Department of Commerce, Miscellaneous Series, No. 60, Washington, 1917, p. 214.

resulted that many manufacturers who used the older processes were in locations sufficiently favorable on account of proximity to customers to balance completely or partially the lower cost of manufacture on the Owens machine. The result was that the machine was introduced more slowly than it would have been if it had been leased or sold to all factories which desired its use.

(2) The great mass of glass jars and bottles are bought by manufacturers and dealers for use as containers for other commodities. When bottles are made by hand, the extra expense involved in having a specially designed bottle, even when ordered in limited quantities, is not large. It came about, therefore, that the purchaser of jars and bottles used them as part of the machinery of his advertising. Shape, markings, and even color were combined to give distinctive appearance to the bottle. Many of the articles put up in glass containers have a small market, and the orders of the makers of these articles are for only a small number of bottles. The Owens machine is an instrument of large-scale production, and the manufacturers who were using the older methods of manufacture — hand and semi-automatic — were able, therefore, to hold the orders for small lots of special bottles. This advantage has been less important in recent years, as the small user of glass containers, in order to secure cheaper bottles, has become willing to use standard sizes and shapes and to rely on the label for his distinctive mark.

(3) The third obstacle to the more rapid encroachment of the Owens machine on the older processes was the development of the semi-automatic machines in range and efficiency. The original machines of this type could be used only for the manufacture of wide-mouth ware, and required for their operation two skilled workers — the gatherer and the presser. As early as 1906,

manufacturers began to equip the machines with cut-offs, displacing the pressers; the labor cost was thus nearly halved. About 1908, semi-automatic machines for making narrow-mouth ware, such as beer and catsup bottles, began to come into use. The earliest of these machines were operated by three men, but they were rapidly improved, and first, two-man machines, and later, one-man machines were introduced. By 1917 almost all semi-automatic machines were operated by one man. All these developments were helpful in enabling the manufacturer who did not have Owens machines to reduce his labor cost.

The following table compiled from the reports of the Glass Bottle Blowers' Association shows the rapid growth in the number of semi-automatic machines. The figures are only for union factories and, since an increasing proportion of all semi-automatic machines came under control of the union during the period under review, they slightly exaggerate the rate of increase.

NUMBER OF SEMI-AUTOMATIC BOTTLE MACHINES AND OPERATORS, 1906–17

	Number of wide-mouth machines	Number of narrow-mouth machines	Numbers of operators
1906	168	...	630
1907	191	...	710
1908	223	...	830
1909	205	19	944
1910	216	...	..
1911	173	52	1,004
1912	170	96*	..
1913	201	96*	..
1914	210	102*	..
1915	193	265	1,700†
1916	167	292	2,000†
1917	428		2,000†

* The figures for narrow-mouth machines in 1912, 1913, and 1914 include only machines of the older type—the three-man machine. The increasing number of one-man and two-man machines was not included until 1915.

† Partially estimated.

(4) The fourth factor in preventing a more rapid engrossment of the trade by the Owens machine was the necessity of adapting the machine to different types of ware. The machine was successful from the outset in manufacturing heavy jars and bottles, but its adaptation to light-weight bottles required time. Until 1912 the greater part of prescription bottles — amounting to one fourth of the total production in quantity and one third in value — were made by hand. The first attempts to manufacture this class of ware on the Owens machine were not successful, but by 1915 the problem was completely solved. In 1917, licenses were granted by the Owens Company for the manufacture of carboys and other large-size bottles.

III

In 1907, when the Owens machine began to be important as a factor in the production of bottles, nearly nine tenths of the hand blowers and operators of semi-automatic machines in the United States were members of the Glass Bottle Blowers' Association. There were some non-union factories, and in some factories the semi-automatic machines were under the jurisdiction of the Flint Glass Workers' Union, but neither class was important. Throughout the period from 1907 to 1917 the Association not only maintained, but even increased, its hold over both hand blowers and semi-automatic machine operators.

Over a period of many years, the Blowers have built up an elaborate system of national collective bargaining with the Association of Bottle Manufacturers. Two conferences are held each year. At the preliminary conference, in May, tentative proposals for changes in wages and rules are made, but no final decision on any question is reached. In July the union holds its annual convention, and the delegates express their opinion on matters affecting the trade. At the final conference, in August, the wages are fixed and rules laid down for the coming "blast." It is a recognized principle that neither the union nor the employers can legislate separately as to matters affecting the trade. The union, therefore, can pass no rules as to hours or apprenticeship; it can only propose such rules to the conference. If the final conference adjourns without an agreement, neither side is bound to observe any of the rules adopted in previous years.

The formulation of a machine policy by the union was of necessity slow, since the range of the Owens machine was only gradually ascertained. In 1904, President Hayes discussed the possible effects of the machine, then in an experimental stage. He was convinced that it could make beer bottles very cheaply, and that the future of the 1600 members of the union who were making such bottles was in jeopardy. He reckoned, however, that it would be two or three years before enough machines could be put into operation to affect these workmen very seriously, and counted on a sufficient enlargement of demand in other divisions of the trade to afford them employment. In his tentative plan for meeting any further encroachment, emphasis was put on the adoption of a three-shift system in order to divide work among the blowers.[1] The introduction of three shifts was to be delayed, however, until unemployment appeared, since the innovation would spend its force as a remedy in its introduction. In 1905, President Hayes was still convinced that the field for the Owens machine was limited to heavy-weight bottles.[2] He urged, however, that the number of apprentices should be reduced as a precautionary measure. In 1907, when the semi-

1. Proceedings, Glass Bottle Blowers, 1904, pp. 39, 40.
2. Ibid., 1905, p. 62.

automatic machine for making narrow-mouth bottles began to come into use, President Hayes counselled the union to make generous terms for it, as a competitor of the Owens employing skilled men. Until 1909 the officers of the union steadily opposed the reduction in the scale for hand workers, as a means of coping with the Owens machine, but in that year a considerable reduction was made.

The policy of the union, as finally formulated in 1909 and consistently pursued thereafter, was composed, therefore, of four parts: (1) the introduction of the three-shift system, (2) the reduction in the number of apprentices, (3) the encouragement of the introduction of semi-automatic machines, and (4) the reduction in the piece price of bottles made by hand.

(1) At the time the Owens machine was introduced, the two-shift system was in common use in glass-bottle factories. The actual working time of each shift was eight and one half hours, but the men stopped an hour for dinner and also rested for two periods of fifteen minutes each. The factory was thus open for twenty hours of the twenty-four, and work was going on for seventeen hours. Since the chief purpose of the proposed three-shift system was to divide the work among a larger number of blowers, the union wished at the time of its introduction to secure also a substantial shortening in the length of the working day. Under the union's three-shift plan the actual working time of each shift was to be seven hours, and an hour was to be taken for dinner.[3] In 1910, when unemployment in the trade was very great, President Hayes decided that the supreme moment, for which the three-shift system had been held in reserve, had arrived, and urged its general adoption.[4]

3. Proceedings, Glass Bottle Blowers, 1907, p. 222.
4. Blowers' Report of the Final Conference, 1910, p. 22.

Altho many of the employers were convinced of the economy of continuous operation, they objected to a generally binding rule on two grounds. In the first place, it was claimed, many of the furnaces were so constructed as to make their continuous operation impossible. Secondly, it was said that it would be difficult to get a sufficient supply of boy helpers for three shifts. Some of the manufacturers suggested that a three-shift system of six-hour shifts would accomplish the desired division of labor and at the same time be workable under existing technical and labor conditions. The conditions varied so much in different factories and localities that it was found impracticable to formulate a binding rule acceptable to both sides, or even to agree on any general rule as to the hours of work where the three-shift system was voluntarily introduced. The union held out for seven hours of work, with an hour for dinner; while the employers, anxious for continuous production, urged that the dinner time should be reduced to half an hour, and that the working week should begin at midnight on Sunday instead of 7 A.M. on Monday.

The same divergence of opinion manifested itself at later conferences. From 1912, however, a provision was inserted in the agreement covering hand blowers, that "where there are a sufficient number of competent idle men and the Branch so requests, every effort shall be made by the manufacturers to employ three shifts. Where there are a number of competent idle men and not enough to operate three shifts, manufacturers and the Committee shall use every effort to arrange for a division of work and time with the idle men." There is no exact information as to how far local unions were able to divide employment by these means, but the reports to the union show that some hand factories did run for periods on the three-shift system. Apparently, however, the greater part of the division of the work actually accomplished was brought about by dividing time with the idle men.

In 1911, the union secured the adoption by the conference of a rule regulating the hours of work where semi-automatic machines were worked on a three-shift system. The length of the shift was to be eight hours with a half-hour out for dinner. The introduction of the three-shift system on the machine was of no effect as a remedy for the unemployment of the hand blowers, but it did reduce the overhead cost of the manufacturers who used semi-automatic machines. Some of the shift-systems introduced in formal compliance with the rule were by no means satisfactory.[5] In some factories, for instance, the three shifts worked four hours on and eight off; in others, four shifts of six hours were worked.

(2) The system of apprenticeship for blowers, in force when the Owens machine was introduced, was largely the outgrowth of custom and had been changed very little by the conference. As custom had shaped the institution, an apprentice served five years, and during this period was paid one half the piece price for journeymen. In 1902 the term of service was fixed by the conference at fifty months of working time — the practical equivalent of five years. From the inception of the system of agreements, the number of apprentices to be taken has been decided annually by the conference, the usual allowance being one to fifteen. It was recognized that the apprentice after a year's service produced about as much ware as a journeyman, and was therefore profitable to the employer.[6] Moreover, the hand factories, and to a less extent the hand-machine factories, required a number of boys as auxiliary workers, and the

5. Proceedings, Glass Bottle Blowers, 1917, p. 165.
6. Report of the Industrial Commission, 1901, vol. vii, p. 110.

prospect of becoming a blower was a strong inducement to boys to enter the factories. The employers were always, therefore, anxious to have a high ratio of apprentices.

The union officials argued at the annual conferences from 1905 to 1907 that in view of the increase in the number of Owens machines the allowance of apprentices should be reduced. They were faced, however, by the fact that all available bottle blowers were fully employed. In 1907 the union was extremely anxious to keep the apprentice ratio low and offered to loan apprentices on the next year's ratio, but the employers were unwilling to accept this compromise and obtained an increase in the ratio to one to ten.[7] In 1908, however, when a large number of bottle blowers were unemployed, the union secured a reduction in the ratio to one to fifteen, and from 1909 made a reduction in the number of apprentices a cardinal part of its machine policy. The union conferees secured the insertion of a provision in the annual agreement for 1909–10 that no apprentices should be taken. In 1912, the union again secured an agreement that no apprentices should be taken.

By this time the union had become keenly aware that the continuing obstacle to a radical restriction in the number of apprentices was the financial advantage to the employer in taking apprentices. Experience had shown that the apprenticeship ratio could be discussed only in connection with wages. In 1905, for example,

7. "The workers proceeded to illustrate to the Manufacturers that in the face of the introduction of automatic machinery we were confronted with the prospect of a surplus of idle men, should the machine be installed as rapidly as indicated, which would place us in a rather peculiar position. While the state of the trade and glass market continued in its present good condition, we could not supply the employers with sufficient blowers to man their plants, but to increase the number of apprentices at this time, should there come a period of depression, would leave us with a number of surplus men with no work." Blowers' Report of Final Conference, 1907, p. 29.

the employers had offered to take no apprentices if they were given a reduction of 15 per cent in wages. In 1909 and 1912, the only two years in which the union had secured an agreement to take no apprentices, heavy reductions in wages had been granted.[8] Accordingly, in 1913, the union insisted on a radical change in the apprenticeship rule. It was agreed that the term of the apprentice should be four years — 40 working months — and that he should be paid 75 per cent of the journeyman's piece price. There was thus left to the employer very little advantage in taking apprentices. From 1913 the apprenticeship question lost its importance, largely because the union was convinced that under the new rule the employer would not take apprentices unless there was a scarcity of journeymen.

(3) The development of the semi-automatic machine was regarded favorably by the union, since the operators were usually recruited from the blowers.[9] From one point of view, the machine caused displacement, since the production for each operator was far greater than the amount made by a hand blower.[1] On the other hand, since the kind of ware which was made on the semi-automatic machines could also be made on the Owens machine, there was offered at least a prospect of skilled employment.

The officers of the union, therefore, welcomed the advent of the newer forms of the semi-automatic machines. In 1908, President Hayes, in reporting to the convention

8. In 1909, the Manufacturers' offer of settlement contained the following clause: "That no apprentices be taken for the blast of 1909–10 and to prevent this increasing the net cost of ware, a reduction of 10 per cent be allowed on all other ware except . . ." Manufacturers' Report of Final Conference, 1909, p. 7.

9. "The Introduction of Semi-Automatic Bottle Machinery," p. 71.

1. The most efficient form of the semi-automatic machine produces approximately four times as much in the same length of time as four hand blowers, and is operated by one skilled man.

the attempts then being made to introduce the narrow-mouth machine, said: "If its operation is such as to encourage manufacturers to believe that with it they can hold their trade against the Owens automatic, then it will become a factor of some consequence in the machine problem." In 1910, in replying to members of the union who complained that the scale made for the narrow-mouth machine was too low, President Hayes said: "If the price list is raised on the machine, I fear it will furnish its competitors, especially those operating the automatic, with a chance to put it out of existence. It would not be good policy at this time to place any obstructions in the way of a machine that employs our men." As the machines became more productive the low piece rates originally fixed yielded a larger daily wage. The union, moreover, took advantage of the introduction of the two-man and one-man machines to secure more remunerative piece rates. By 1914 the average daily wages of machine operators were about equal to those of hand blowers, and by 1917 they were somewhat larger.

(4) The final part of the union's machine policy was the reduction in the piece rates for hand blowers. At the beginning, this form of defence against displacement was not favored. President Hayes, in 1905, in reply to the arguments of the manufacturers that a reduction in prices was necessary in order to keep work from the Owens machine, said: "The automatic machine is coming without question and it will not be long until glass houses will look more like machine shops, and glass blowers will lose their jobs, but he believed they will be able to obtain other jobs. Whether they do or not, he insisted that no reduction in wages could stop the introduction of the machines." [2] From 1905 to 1908 the

2. Manufacturers' Report of the Final Wage Conference, 1905, p. 31.

union held tenaciously to this position. Even in 1908, when many blowers were idle, President Hayes said at the final conference that he could not "see how a reduction in wages, even tho applied to certain brackets, would help the situation, either for the manufacturer or for the blowers at the present time." [3]

The long depression in the trade in 1908–09 and a threatened disruption of the conference system brought a change in the attitude, if not in the opinion, of the leaders of the union. When the final conference was held in 1909 they were prepared to submit to a reduction. The employers urged a general reduction of 50 per cent, and in support of their proposal developed an ingenious theory. "Almost all machines," they said in substance, "go through a lengthy period of experimentation. When the wages of the hand workers are high, the machines are able to run during this period at a profit; later, they are perfected. If the wages of hand workers were lower, the machines would not be profitable in their experimental form, and would be abandoned. The proper policy is to reduce wages, not only on ware already being made on the machine, but also on ware to which the machine is not yet adapted."

The leaders of the union were opposed to any reduction on classes of bottles not then being made on the machine, and maintained vigorously that "lowering wages has never stopped the invention of machinery." However, they were willing to make reductions on lines of ware which were being made on the Owens machine, not because they believed that such reductions would keep any considerable amount of work for a long time from the machine, but because they wished to hold together the conference. If some concession were not made in wages, it was almost certain that the confer-

3. Manufacturers' Report of the Final Wage Conference, 1908, p. 38.

ence would disintegrate. In that event, the union officials, with three thousand hand blowers unemployed, were doubtful of their ability to enforce the scale and rules. Ultimately an agreement was reached, under which a 20 per cent reduction was conceded on the piece price of "beers, sodas, etc., 10 oz. weight and over," one of 20 per cent on "brandies, catsups, etc., 8 oz. and over," and one of 10 per cent on "liquor ovals, 6 oz. and over." The first two classes included ware which the machine had been producing successfully, while the third class was ware on which the machine only recently had begun to encroach. The union refused to make any concession in the piece price for prescription bottles and other classes of ware which the machine was not making.

The policy established by the union in 1909 was followed thereafter whenever it was impossible to avoid a reduction. In 1910 and 1911 the union was able to hold the conference together without any lowering of wage rates. By 1912, however, the situation was again beyond control and some reduction was necessary. The union finally agreed to take a discount of 20 per cent on all ware then being made on the machine. This involved a heavy total reduction — amounting to 38 per cent — on ware which had already been reduced in 1909. By the time the conference was held in 1914, the Owens machine was making small ware successfully. The union conferees accordingly agreed to accept reductions of 20 per cent on the small sizes of ware. Only one of the greater "brackets" into which bottles and jars are ordinarily classified — "toilets and colognes" — remained exclusively hand-made, and the prices for this ware accordingly were still left at the "net" list — that is, at the price paid in 1907. The reduction in 1914 was the last made with the avowed purpose of meeting the competition of the Owens machine.

The advisability of these reductions was warmly debated. The advocates of reduction claimed that the difference in the cost of production, including return on investment, between machine and hand methods was not large and that by moderate reductions the union could equalize the cost. Those who opposed any concession based their argument on the assertion that the manufacturers who were using the Owens machine had not reduced the prices of bottles. Neither side was able to support its case by detailed evidence. The total cost of production on Owens machines was known only to the users, and there were no available figures of bottle prices. Experience showed, however, that the reductions had no appreciable effect in preventing displacement. Here and there a hand manufacturer was able to continue in business a little longer or delayed installing semi-automatic machines for a time, because of the reductions. But these were minor results.

In the foregoing review, it will be noted, pressure to secure the employment of hand blowers as attendants on Owens machines is not enumerated as part of the union's policy. In view of the fact that the demand for the employment of displaced hand blowers as operators had been the central point in the policy of the union in dealing with semi-automatic machines, it may appear curious that the same rule was not adopted for the Owens machine. There were two reasons. In the first place, the number of displaced hand blowers who could have been placed in this way was almost negligible. Secondly, the disparity in the wage of hand blowers and of machine attendants was too great. The attendants on the Owens machines are unskilled workers, and the manufacturer would have been unwilling to pay them a wage comparable to that earned by hand blowers and operators of semi-automatic machines. In 1906, for example, when hand blowers were earning seven dollars a day, and machine men four to five dollars, the attendants on the Owens machine were receiving twenty cents per hour.[4] In 1915, in pursuance of a plan for organizing all workers in glass-bottle factories, the union secured an agreement with the American Bottle Company, the largest user of Owens machines, under which the Company gave jurisdiction over its machine attendants and packers to the Blowers. It was also provided that preference in employment should be given to displaced hand blowers. This agreement, however, is the only one of its kind. In most Owens factories there are some displaced blowers working as attendants, but their employment has been due to the fact that the plant is in the town where they formerly worked as hand blowers, and not to any rule or policy of the union.

IV

The effects of the introduction of the Owens machine on the blowers may be grouped under three heads: (1) wages, (2) displacement, and (3) the loss of the summer stop.

(1) In 1905 the wages of blowers relatively to wages in other skilled trades were very high. There were great differences in the piece earnings on different classes of bottles, but it would not be an extravagant estimate to put the earnings in the trade as a whole at an average of seven dollars per day.[5] The reductions made in 1909,

4. Proceedings, Glass Bottle Blowers, 1906, p. 30.

5. In testifying before the Commission on Industrial Relations in 1914, Mr. Hayes, President of the Blowers, said: "Our men made good wages before the reductions. The glass blowers made from $6 to $18 and $20 per day. Of course, they were only the exceptions — the $18 and $20 men. That was for carboys and demijohns. But $8 and $10 were

1912, and 1914, did not affect average earnings nearly as much as they would have done if they had been made at an earlier period. For example, if a blower in 1915 had made beer bottles, he would have received less than two thirds of the piece price of 1908, but relatively few beer bottles were made by hand blowers in 1915. In 1914 President Hayes estimated the average wage of blowers at $4.50 to $5.00,[6] and in 1916 and 1917 considerable increases were secured. It would not be wide of the mark, therefore, to estimate the average wages of hand blowers in 1917 at $6.00 per day. Compared with the movements of wages in other organized trades, the bottle blowers lost more heavily. The index number of union wage rates, compiled by the Bureau of Labor Statistics, shows an increase for this period in hourly rates of wages from 100 to 127.[7] Those blowers who secured employment on the semi-automatic machines, in one sense, fared better. While their wages were lower than the wages of blowers in 1907, by 1917 they were slightly higher.

(2) From 1907 to 1917, not less than one half of the hand blowers employed in the former year lost positions of skill and passed into unskilled work. The following table, compiled from the reports of the union, shows the total working force — that is, apprentices and journeymen together — in factories under the jurisdiction of the Glass Bottle Blowers, on March 1, for each year from 1905 to 1917: [8]

about the average wages for a glass bottle blower." Report of Commission on Industrial Relations, vol. 3, p. 3016. Other evidence, such, for example, as an elaborate inquiry of the manufacturers in 1900, indicates that President Hayes' estimate was somewhat too high.

6. Report of Commission on Industrial Relations, vol. 3, p. 3016.

7. "Union Scale of Wages and Hours of Labor, 1923," Bulletin No. 354, p. 22.

8. I am indebted for these figures, as well as for much other information, to Mr. Harry Jenkins, Secretary of the Glass Bottle Blowers' Association.

1905	8,000	1912	7,703
1906	8,559	1913	7,703
1907	9,627	1914	6,868
1908	8,822	1915	4,941
1909	7,005	1916	5,314
1910	7,634	1917	6,321
1911	7,477		

For the present purpose, one important correction must be made in these figures. In 1914 the union, which had included theretofore only skilled workers, began to organize packers and other unskilled laborers. In 1915, under an agreement with the American Bottle Company, 500 machine attendants, packers, and other unskilled workers were taken into membership. In 1916 and 1917 the general organization of packers was vigorously undertaken. The increase in working force under union control from 1915 to 1917 does not represent, therefore, an increase in skilled workers. On the contrary, there was some loss in these years. The number of skilled workers — hand blowers and semi-automatic machine workers — may be estimated approximately at 4000 in 1917.

The displacement of blowers, it will be noted from the table, was by no means at an equal annual rate. The periods of great displacement correspond to the steps in the adaptation of the machine to the various classes of bottles. The period from 1905 to 1907 was one of rapid growth in employment. The number of Owens machines was increasing, but not so rapidly as the demand for bottles. So urgent was the demand for workers in 1907 that the union agreed to loan on the next year's quota of apprentices. In his annual report in 1907, President Hayes said, "The year just closed has been a phenomenal one in the glass trade." In the peak year 1907, the working force of skilled men in union factories was 9627; in 1909 it was 7005 — a fall of 2600.

Some recovery came in 1910, and until 1913 no further fall in total working force was experienced. The second great period of displacement began in 1913 and was due to the extension of the range of the machine to small light-weight bottles. The working force of skilled workers fell from 7703 in 1913 to approximately 4000 in 1917, a loss of 3700.[9]

Even during the periods of largest displacement, there were constant complaints from the manufacturers of a scarcity of hand blowers. To some extent this curious condition was due to the fact that many blowers had specialized in making particular lines of ware, and when their branch of the trade passed to the machine, were unable to do satisfactory work in any of the remaining branches. Moreover, the glass-bottle industry has never been concentrated in a few large centers. When the Owens machines were installed in a factory, therefore, opportunities for employment at hand blowing in the same locality were not open. Family ties, ownership of a house, or some other impediment to mobility led many of the displaced blowers to relinquish the trade permanently.

The Blowers have never had an unemployment benefit, and such relief as had been given prior to 1909 was given entirely by local unions. In the autumn of 1908 the executive officers began making loans to branches to assist them in aiding the unemployed and, in January, 1909, levied an assessment of 5 per cent on the earnings of employed members. To August 1, 1909, a total of $266,000 from this source was paid. Married men were given seven dollars per week and unmarried men five dollars. In 1912, again, the national union made loans to branches.

9. Both of these estimates of the amount of displacement are made on the assumption that the number of apprentices taken was adequate to offset the natural loss in a stationary trade.

(3) Almost from the beginning of their organization, the Blowers had enforced an annual stop of two months — July and August. The summer stop was an inconvenience to the manufacturers, as it made necessary the stocking of ware. But since the rule was uniformly binding on all union factories, it was observed without much complaint. With the introduction of the Owens machines, which ran the year round, strong opposition to the summer stop developed on the part of the hand and semi-automatic machine manufacturers, who were placed at a serious competitive disadvantage, since they or their customers must store bottles, and run the chance of having an insufficient supply. The amount used of many kinds of bottles varies widely from one year to another, according to the crop yield or according to the heat of the summer. It is an important advantage to the users of these classes of bottles to be able to order a supplementary supply. In 1908 the union conceded to the manufacturers who used semi-automatic machines the privilege of running all summer. This action was forced on the Blowers by a similar concession on the part of the Flint Glass Workers, who then controlled a small section of the semi-automatic machine operators. The hand manufacturers demanded the same privilege, but the union refused to yield anything until 1912, when an agreement was reached, under which the summer stop was fixed at one month for hand factories and at two weeks for machine plants.

The manufacturers were strongly of the opinion that even the modified summer stop left them at a great disadvantage in competition with the factories that used Owens machines, and constantly urged the abolition of the summer stop. A compromise was reached in 1917, when continuous operation was allowed, but it was agreed that each blower was to take a compulsory vacation for four consecutive weeks, and each machine operator, for two consecutive weeks, between June 15 and September 15. The strong opposition on the part of the union to yielding the summer stop has been due chiefly to the reluctance of the men to work in the intense heat of the factories during the summer. But the summer suspension also is regarded as one method of dividing up the available work among a larger number of men, and thus reducing the amount of displacement.

B. The Introduction of Flow and Feed Devices

For a number of years, the Owens was the only automatic machine widely used in the manufacture of bottles and jars.[1] Numerous attempts were made to devise a mechanism for automatically withdrawing glass from the tank by other means than the suction method, which had been successfully applied in the Owens machine. As early as 1903, Brooke devised a machine descriptively known as the "flowing device." There were technical difficulties to be overcome, however, and only a small part of the total production of bottles was made by flow and feed devices until about 1917. By that time, a number of different types of these devices were being marketed.

The advantages of the flow and feed devices over the semi-automatic machines are very great. In the first place, the labor cost is much reduced, since a flow and feed device produces approximately twice as much as the best form of semi-automatic machine, and is watched by an attendant who is paid at a rate not much higher than the rate for unskilled labor. Secondly, the

1. In 1912, the Hazel-Atlas Glass Company was using a pouring device, which produced certain classes of jars satisfactorily. Proceedings, Glass Bottle Blowers, 1912, p. 102.

device is ordinarily worked continuously except for the Sunday intermission. Thirdly, the bottles produced are more uniform in weight and content than those made by the most skilled operators of semi-automatic machines.

It is impossible to secure any direct statistical information as to the rate of introduction of flow and feed devices, since they are made by a number of different companies. Moreover, in many cases the device feeds more than one machine, and the unit of measurement is therefore inexact. But the decline in the number of semi-automatic machines furnishes an index, since the flow and feed device usually replaces the semi-automatic machine. The union, which has had practically complete control over these machines, reports the number in use from 1916 to 1924 as follows:

1916	459	1921	288
1917	428	1922	164
1918	417	1923	130
1919	..	1924	72
1920	315		

From these figures it appears that the period of rapid decline in semi-automatic machines was from 1918 to 1924. The total number of flow and feed devices in operation in 1924 cannot be accurately stated, since the union has jurisdiction over only a part. In that year, the reports showed that the union had jurisdiction over 201 devices, on which 1000 men were employed.[2] The total number of flow and feed devices was not less than 300, and probably more.

The policy of the union with reference to the new machines was not laid down until 1918, because until that

2. The number actually reported in 1924 was 747, but in their reports the local unions did not differentiate completely attendants and machine operators. As a rough approximation, one half of the machine operators have been reclassified as attendants. Proceedings, Glass Bottle Blowers, 1924, p. 33.

time they were operated chiefly in non-union establishments. In 1916 the President of the Association called the attention of the convention to the fact that in four places the new devices were displacing members of the union. At that time, however, semi-automatic machines were increasing in number and machine operators were in demand. The devices, therefore, even in union factories were manned for the most part by unskilled laborers paid at a rate considerably below the wage obtainable by a skilled operator. Some of the displaced machine operators on their own account turned to the new devices, preferring such employment rather than a hazard of fortune in a new place. The wages were much lower, in fact, rarely more than that of a day laborer, but the work was much easier. The strain of piece-work gathering at a wage of $8.00 for an eight-hour day was exchanged in some cases for a twelve-hour day of watching at the rate of 35 cents per hour.[3] The union used its influence at various places where the devices were introduced to secure the employment of the displaced operators. But it made no formal claim of jurisdiction over the attendants, and there was no prescribed wage scale.

In 1918 the union secured an agreement with a few of the manufacturers who were using the devices, and since then it has sought to secure similar agreements with the remainder. This change in policy was due to the rapid introduction of the devices, and the consequent decrease in the number of semi-automatic machines. The displaced operators were now usually desirous of work-

3. In 1918, one of the executives of the union, in describing a newly installed plant at Kansas City, said: "The two (flow and feed devices) were feeding six machines. Three of our members were working around these machines. There were about eight men employed, of whom five did not belong to our organization. . . . These men were working 12 hours a day for 35 cents per hour." Proceedings, Glass Bottle Blowers' Association, 1918, p. 200.

ing as attendants. The agreement made in 1918 has been renewed each year, except in 1921, when it was found impossible to agree on wages. The first agreement provided for a wage of 50 cents per hour; in 1919, this was increased to 60 cents, and in 1920, to 66 cents. In 1921 the employers stood out for a reduction to 50 cents, and no agreement was signed. Since 1922 the minimum hourly rate has been 60 cents. A considerable number of the employers, however, pay above the minimum, either as a flat rate or as a bonus.

The part of the agreement of most interest in the present connection is the provision for employment. It is agreed that "when an operator is to be hired, he shall be a member of the Glass Bottle Blowers' Association, providing said Association shall be able to furnish experienced or satisfactory operators and in case it is not, then help may be drawn from any source . . . and any operator so put up shall at the end of six months be taken into the Association." In 1924 the union attempted to change the provision so as to make it mandatory on the manufacturers in all cases to employ members of the union. This would have made it certain that displaced blowers and operators would be given preference. The manufacturers successfully objected to this change, but asserted that all of them did employ members of the union when available.

It may be estimated roughly that about one third of the 2000 machine operators employed in 1917 have secured employment on flow and feed devices.[4] A few hundred are still employed as machine operators. The policy adopted by the union has been successful in reducing considerably the displacement from the trade. Since the total number of attendants on feed and flow

4. Part of the 1000 union members employed on the devices are unskilled laborers, who have been admitted to the union since their employment as attendants.

devices in 1924, however, was less than the number of machine operators in 1917, a considerable amount of displacement was unavoidable.

The insistence of the union on the employment of displaced blowers and machine operators on the feed and flow device is in marked contrast with its policy with reference to the Owens machine. This is easily explicable. In the first place, as has been noted above, the employment of hand blowers or operators as attendants on the Owens machine would have afforded a negligible amount of employment for the displaced workers. But the feed and flow devices could very well have absorbed one half or more of the displaced operators. Secondly, the disparity in wages between the operator of a semi-automatic machine and an unskilled laborer was very much less in 1918 than it had been in 1907. From 1907 to 1918, the wages of operators rose far less than the wages of unskilled labor. The employers for the most part were willing to pay something more to displaced operators than the price of unskilled labor; the operators were willing to take something less than they had been getting rather than leave the trade. The gap was not too great to be bridged.

The union has been too much engaged with the problem of securing the employment of displaced operators as attendants to give much attention as yet to the conditions of employment other than wages. The flow and feed devices are now usually run on eight-hour shifts, 18 shifts per week. The union has urged the explicit acceptance of the eight-hour day, and the introduction of a 32-hour week-end stop, but it has not been able to secure the acceptance of its proposals.

In the period from 1917 to 1924 the displacement of hand blowers continued. The causes were of several kinds. The adaptation of the Owens machine to the making of large containers was responsible for some displacement. The Eighteenth Amendment reduced the production of bottles one fourth and caused a still heavier loss. Altho beer bottles and liquor flasks in 1917 were chiefly made by the Owens machine, some were still made by hand. Moreover, the reduction in the total output intensified competition in the trade. The growing tendency toward the use of standard bottles also played a part in displacement. In 1924 the number of blowers reported at work in union factories was 749, about one half of the number at work in 1917. Hand blowers in 1924 were chiefly engaged in making "cologne and toilet" bottles. These bottles are of varied sizes and shapes, usually made from closed-pot furnaces, with distinctive decorative features, and ordinarily made in comparatively small lots. Fortunately for the remaining blowers, there has been an increase in the demand for such bottles in recent years.

Under these circumstances, it is not remarkable that the wages of blowers since 1917 have lagged relatively to wages in other trades. In 1924 the officers of the union estimated the average daily wage of a blower at seven dollars — an increase of one dollar over 1917, and about the wage received in 1907.[5] In the meantime, wages in most other trades have advanced much more. If the index number of union wage rates be taken as a criterion, it appears that wages generally rose from 1917 to 1924 about 80 per cent.

From the foregoing account, it is clear that the introduction of automatic machinery in the manufacture

5. The "toilet and cologne" piece-scale of 1924, however, was nearly 50 per cent above that of 1907. The discrepancy is partly due to the fact that in 1907 most of the other brackets were more remunerative than the "toilet and cologne" brackets, while at present the "toilet and cologne" brackets are more remunerative than the others. It is partly accounted for by the reduction in the length of the working-day in 1919 from eight and one half hours to eight.

of glass bottles and jars presented a problem which no trade union policy could have solved completely. Despite an increase of 50 per cent in the production of glass bottles in less than twenty years, the number of men employed in the industry for all work analogous to the original work of the hand blower is less than one third of the number employed in 1907. Moreover, the greater part of this loss was suffered in the nine years from 1908 to 1917. In that time the number of men so employed fell from 10,000 to not more than 4000. No trade union rule, nor any combination of trade union rules, could have prevented a great displacement of skilled labor from the trade.

Under these circumstances, the policy of the Blowers has been controlled in the last resort by the desire to hold the workmen together in an organization and to maintain contractual relations with the employers. Minor criticisms of policies have already been suggested. An earlier reconstruction of an archaic apprenticeship rule would have kept a thousand or more men out of a dwindling handicraft. It is doubtful whether the reductions made in prices served any economic end. But the large justification of the union's concessions lies in the fact that thereby it made possible the effectual carrying into effect of a number of measures — some of them in less desirable form than was theoretically possible, but in the mass capable of producing a considerable effect in lessening the hardship of the transitional period. Despite a succession of invasions by machines, such as, perhaps, no other trade has experienced in recent years, the Blowers are still a union "in being."

CHAPTER V

MACHINERY AND THE DISPLACEMENT OF SKILL

SUMMARY

Definition of displacement of skill, 117. — The factors determining the amount of displacement, 117. — Rapidity of introduction of the machine, 118. — The mobility of labor within the trade, 122. — Effect of the machine in increasing demand for the product, 126. — The labor-displacing power of the machine, 131. — Extent to which the skill of the handworker is useful in the machine process, 132. — Variety of combination of factors, 137.

That machines do not, even at their first introduction, *invariably* throw human labor out of employment, must be admitted; and it has been maintained, by persons very competent to form an opinion on the subject, that they never produce that effect. The solution of this question depends on facts, which, unfortunately, have not yet been collected; and the circumstance of our not possessing the data necessary for the full examination of so important a subject, supplies an additional reason for impressing upon the minds of all who are interested in such inquiries the importance of procuring accurate registries, at various times, of the number of persons employed in particular branches of manufacture, of the number of machines used by them, and of the wages they receive.[1]

SINCE the beginning of the nineteenth century, the effects of machinery on labor have engaged the attention of many economists. The resulting discussion has centered chiefly around two questions: the effect of machinery on the general rate of wages, and the part played by machinery as a cause of unemployment. The present chapter deals with a third effect of machinery, — the displacement of skill.

1. Charles Babbage, Economy of Machinery and Manufactures, Fourth Edition, 1835, pp. 336–337.

By displacement of skill, in the sense in which the term is here used, is meant the loss of the opportunity to sell acquired skill at the rate of remuneration which would have been received if the machine had not been introduced. Displacement, therefore, does not necessarily mean loss of employment. If the employment after the introduction of the machine, and as a consequence thereof, is at a lower rate of remuneration, displacement of skill has occurred. In a skilled trade, there is at any time an amount of skill which may be valued at a certain sum. This sum is the discounted value of all the premiums above the price of unskilled labor which the skilled workmen would have collected if the machine had not been introduced. If any part of this expectation is lost through the introduction of machinery, a displacement of skill has occurred.

The factors determining the extent of the displacement of skill consequent upon the introduction of machinery may be enumerated as follows: (1) the rapidity of introduction of the machine, (2) the mobility of labor within the skilled trade affected, (3) the effect of the machine in reducing the price of the manufactured article and thus increasing demand, (4) the labor-displacing power of the machine, (5) the extent to which the skill of the handworker is useful in the machine process. Altho economic discussion has not been directed in detail to the particular question here considered, many economic writers, in the course of their treatment of the effects of machinery on general wages or on unemployment, have expressed opinions as to the operation of some of these factors. These opinions will be examined under their respective heads. The facts used have been drawn chiefly from the studies of particular cases of the introduction of machinery in skilled trades included in the four preceding chapters.[2] In the present chapter the assumption has been made throughout that economic forces are working on a purely competitive basis. Accordingly, no account has been taken of any form of intervention. The chief modifying force in the working of these factors in the past has been the trade unions of the handworkers. In a final chapter the possibilities and achievements of trade-union intervention will be considered.

I

The assumption that the rate of introduction of machinery was likely to be slow has had a long history in economic writing. J. B. Say laid it down as one of the characteristics of the introduction of machinery, ameliorative in its effect, that "new machines are slowly constructed and still more slowly brought into use." [3] By far the most elaborate development of this doctrine was that of Professor J. S. Nicholson, in his book "The Effects of Machinery on Wages," first published in 1878. Professor Nicholson's "Law of Continuity" is divided into two parts. The first asserts that "a radical change made in the methods of invention will be *gradually and continuously adopted*." [4] More concretely, he says:

> Suppose that a radical change is introduced by some ingenious producer into a certain manufacture which will lead to the employment of less labor. That this process will be adopted in process of time by all other manufacturers is evident, but I maintain that in comparison with the mobility of labor the process will be slow.

2. Chapters I–IV, referred to respectively hereafter by title as "The Introduction of the Linotype," "The Stonecutters' Union and the Stone-Planer," "The Introduction of Semi-Automatic Bottle Machinery," "The Introduction of Automatic Bottle Machines."

3. J. B. Say, A Treatise on Political Economy, New American Edition, Philadelphia, 1848, p. 87.

4. J. S. Nicholson, The Effects of Machinery on Wages, new and revised edition, 1892, p. 33. The italics are Professor Nicholson's.

The second part of the "Law of Continuity" sets forth that "these radical changes tend to give place to advances by small *increases of invention.*" To the same effect is Professor S. J. Chapman's assertion: "New inventions are slowly adopted as a rule, and, at first, owing to their imperfections, the saving in labor effected by them is usually small." [5]

In their discussions, Professor Chapman and Professor Nicholson were concerned chiefly with the effect of machinery on unemployment, but the "Law of Continuity" has a direct relation to displacement of skill. Professor Nicholson recognizes this relationship in the following passage:

> This destruction of the laborer's only capital is one of the most pernicious effects of machinery and when it happens there is and can be no remedy. Still, if the changes are gradual the evil consequences are not so great.[6]

Before considering the possible effects of a slow rate of introduction in conserving skill, it will be convenient to examine the various causes of slowness, since the possibilities of diminishing displacement turn largely upon the character of the retardation.

1. The retarding force on which Professor Nicholson lays greatest emphasis is the inertia of the manufacturer.

> The more enterprising the capitalist [he says], the sooner he will make any change, but the change will not in reference to labor be sudden. . . . The change will at first be adopted by some enterprising capitalist in the centre of a highly competitive region and will gradually extend to the manufactories of less competent masters in more remote districts.[7]

An examination of the history of the introduction of machinery in the glass bottle, printing and stonecutting trades does not confirm the opinion that the retardation

5. S. J. Chapman, Outlines of Political Economy, 1911, p. 84.
6. Nicholson, op. cit., p. 44.
7. Ibid., pp. 36–37.

due to inertia is sufficiently long to be important. On the contrary, it appears that where a machine is sold or leased to any manufacturer willing to pay the price, it is introduced with great rapidity. The stone-planer was fully introduced in about seven years; the period of introduction of the linotype did not cover more than ten years; the number of narrow-mouth semi-automatic bottle machines did not increase much after six years; the "flow and feed" devices for making bottles were fully introduced in five years.[8] In all these cases there was some increase in the number of machines after the period of introduction, but it was due to expansion in production and not to the displacement of the hand process.

2. The second cause of slowness of introduction, noted both by Professor Nicholson and by Professor Chapman, is the increasing capacity of the machines, partly because of improvements in the construction of the machine and partly because of the greater speed of the operatives. In the machines studied, this factor was of great importance. The first operators of the linotype produced much less than the present operators. The stone-planer was improved in speed by various modifications of its form and a great increase secured in output per man employed. The semi-automatic bottle machine gained in efficiency over a considerable period of time. The capacity of the Owens bottle machine more than trebled in ten years. Less important yet notable improvements have been made in "flow and feed" devices for the automatic manufacture of glass bottles.[9]

8. "The Stonecutters' Union and the Stone-Planer," pp. 31–32; "The Introduction of the Linotype," p. 3; "The Introduction of Semi-Automatic Bottle Machinery," p. 69; "The Introduction of Automatic Bottle Machines," p. 110.

9. "The Introduction of the Linotype," p. 7; "The Stonecutters' Union and the Stone-Planer," p. 32; "The Introduction of Automatic Bottle Machines," pp. 89–92.

3. A third cause of slowness in the introduction of machines is the necessity of adapting the machine to the various products made by the skilled handworker. It must be an extremely rare case in which machinery has superseded an entire skilled trade. The scope of the machine, even when it reaches its fullest development, is almost always narrower than the entire handicraft. The extension of the machine to its final limit of performance usually requires time. The early stone-planers covered much less of the stonecutters' original trade than the more recent forms. The present type-setting and type-casting machines have a wider range than the earlier forms. Machinery for making glass bottles originally made only wide-mouth heavy ware. The scope of the machines was gradually extended to other forms of ware, but the period of extension was a long one, reaching from 1895 to 1917.[1]

4. A final cause of retardation, in the introduction of some machines, is the restriction placed on the use of the machine by the patentee in order to profit more largely by his invention. From this point of view, machines may be divided broadly into two classes, accordingly as the patentee, on the one hand, sells or leases the machine to any one who will pay the price or, on the other hand, retains entirely the use of the machine or sells exclusive rights to particular manufacturers. In the latter case, the manufacturers using the machine may prefer to make larger profits on part of the total production, rather than to lower prices sufficiently to drive out competitors using inferior forms of production. This form of retardation can never outlast the patent rights, and may be terminated sooner by the invention of another machine, or a change of policy on the part of the manu-

1. "The Stonecutters' Union and the Stone-Planer," p. 32; "The Introduction of Automatic Bottle Machines," pp. 93–94.

facturer. The policy of selling rights to manufacture particular kinds of bottles to selected manufacturers was pursued by the Owens Bottle Company. The policy of retaining the use of its own machines has been followed by the American Window Glass Company.[2] In both cases, a very considerable retardation in the introduction of the machines resulted.

From the foregoing, it may be concluded that the introduction of machinery is rarely, if ever, catastrophic, and that a considerable period is likely to elapse before the machine has reached its limits as a potential force in displacing skill. Does the existence of this period lessen the total amount of displacement?

II

The extent to which slowness of introduction salvages skill depends on the degree to which the inflow of labor into the hand trade is stopped, and the existing skill utilized to fill available positions.[3] Whether inflow is stopped or checked depends in turn chiefly on whether the skilled labor in the trade is sufficiently mobile. In any particular case, there may be other factors in checking inflow, such as trade-union action, or there may be factors promoting inflow, such as the desire to profit by

2. "Introduction of Automatic Bottle Machines," pp. 90–91; The Glass Industry as affected by the War, Tariff Information Series, No. 5, p. 139.

3. Professor Chapman in dealing with the problem of unemployment as an effect of machinery, where the same reasoning is pertinent, appears to assume that inflow would cease automatically. He says, "Moreover it must be remembered that a re-direction of the labor of the rising generation alone can bring about great changes rapidly, especially in a growing society. An unrecruited industry shrinks at an increasing pace and in a decade its shrinkage must be considerable. The amount of labor displacement, if any, caused by new machinery depends upon the rate at which new machinery is introduced." Chapman, Outlines of Political Economy, p. 84.

apprentices. Generally speaking, however, the effective check to inflow is the mobility of the existing skill in the trade.

The immobility of skilled labor takes various forms. Almost every trade is split up into specialized sections, either coöperant or independent, passage from one to another of which may be difficult. Workmen may prefer to forego the exercise of their skilled trades rather than to incur the disadvantages involved in removal to other localities. The older workmen find great difficulty in learning the operation of the new machines even when the skill of the handworker is wanted for the operation of the machines. Not infrequently two of these three primary obstacles to mobility are combined against the movement of a single workman.

If machines were introduced piece-meal, that is, if an employer installed one machine and then later another, in the meantime having identical work done by hand, the stopping of inflow into the trade would naturally result from the introduction of machines, since an employer ordinarily would not train new workmen when there was already a sufficient supply. But the introduction of machinery does not proceed in this manner. Usually machinery is introduced completely in a single plant, that is, all work of the same kind is done by machine and not part by machine and part by hand. There is bound to be a surplus of skilled workmen at that point, to be absorbed in some other factory in the same kind of skilled work, or in the same factory in some coöperant form of handwork or in working the machine. If they are not thus employed, skill is displaced.

It is entirely conceivable, therefore, that slowness of introduction may have no effect in lessening the displacement of skilled labor. Unless the men thrown out by the machine secure employment in one of the three ways enumerated, slowness of introduction would not affect the total amount of displacement. The persons affected, of course, would not be identical with those who would have been displaced by a more rapid introduction. Many of those in the trade at the time of the first introduction of machinery would be able to exercise their skill for a longer period of time, but the persons entering the trade thereafter would suffer displacement, as a group, in an amount equal to that salvaged by their predecessors.

The influence of mobility in lessening the amount of displacement is not limited by slowness of introduction. Where the skill of the handworker is useful in the machine process, either as a coöperant handworker or as a machine operator, the ability of workers already in the trade to shift to these positions is a factor in the avoidance of displacement.[4]

Illustrations of the effect of immobility on the amount of displacement may be drawn from the history of the introduction of machinery in various trades. The introduction of the linotype was accompanied by conditions highly favorable to the avoidance of displacement of skill. The increase in the demand for printed matter after a short time was great; skilled printers were used as operators for the machines. Skilled men were used as coöperant workers. The total number of skilled workers in the trade steadily increased. Even under these conditions, there was a considerable amount of displacement. The older hand compositors were generally not able to secure employment as machine operators, and there was a surplus of the particular specialized form of skill which they possessed. The younger men were drawn into machine work from other branches in the trade. The places thus vacated were filled to some ex-

4. See below, pp. 133, 135.

tent by men who had been displaced by the machine, but chiefly by an increased inflow into the trade.[5]

The introduction of the semi-automatic bottle machine presents a similar case. The machine was capable of making only wide-mouth bottles; the remainder of the trade was entirely unaffected. During the whole period of its introduction there was a constant and large increase in the total number of glass-bottle blowers, but the displacement of skill was considerable. Many of the men who formerly had made wide-mouth bottles were not able to make satisfactorily other forms of bottles, or were unwilling to remove to the places where such bottles were made. The inflow into the other branches of the trade was sufficiently enlarged to furnish the needed workers.[6]

The introduction of the Owens bottle machine was characterized by displacement of the same kind. As the machine successively invaded various parts of the trade, the transfer of the workers supplanted by the machine to the unaffected branches was very imperfectly accomplished. From 1905 to 1917, the total number of skilled blowers and machine operators fell from 9000 to 4000, yet in most of these years the influx of apprentices was considerable.[7] In the case of the stone-planer the displacement of skill was increased by a change in the location of the industry, as the hand work supplementary to the machine, to a very considerable extent, was transferred to the quarries. The migration of stonecutters to these centers, while large, was insufficient to fill the need, and an inflow into the trade resulted at the very time when stonecutters were being displaced at other points.[8]

5. "The Introduction of the Linotype," p. 18.
6. "The Introduction of Semi-Automatic Bottle Machinery," p. 71.
7. "The Introduction of Automatic Bottle Machines," pp. 99, 107.
8. "The Stonecutters' Union and the Stone-Planer," pp. 62–63.

III

Very early in the discussion of the effect of machinery on the general rate of wages, the apologists of the machine began to argue that the machine by cheapening the price of goods caused such a large increase in consumption as to increase rather than to lessen the demand for labor. J. B. Say appears to have originated this argument. He said:

> The multiplication of a product commonly reduces its price, that reduction extends its consumption; and so its production, tho become more rapid, nevertheless gives employment to more hands than before.[9]

Say was careful to distinguish this as an ultimate and not an immediate effect.

The doctrine was stated very broadly by most of the English economists of this period. Even Malthus, who was careful to assert the possibility of exceptions, said:

> When a machine is invented, which, by saving labor will bring goods into the market at a much cheaper rate than before, the most usual effect is such an extension of the demand for the commodity, by its being brought within the power of a much greater number of purchasers, that the value of the whole mass of goods made by the new machinery greatly exceeds their former value; and, notwithstanding the saving of labor, more hands, instead of fewer, are required in the manufacture.[1]

McCulloch, while denying that the effect of machinery in increasing the production of goods had anything to do with the advantages of machinery, did not hesitate to assert that

> any considerable reduction in the price of a commodity in general use, has uniformly almost been found to extend the demand for it in a much greater proportion.[2]

---

9. Say, A Treatise on Political Economy, New American Edition, 1848, p. 88.

1. T. R. Malthus, Principles of Political Economy, Second Edition, 1836, p. 352.

2. J. R. McCulloch, Principles of Political Economy, Second Edition, 1830, p. 189.

Babbage appears to have been the first English writer of importance to express a doubt as to the "usualness" of an increase in employment consequent upon the introduction of machinery. In a cautious and hesitating chapter, he asserted that "the solution of this question depends on facts which unfortunately have not been collected." He submitted data collected by himself from various sources as to the actual increase in employment in cotton manufacture, but reached no definite conclusion.[3] Mill was equally cautious:

> I cannot assent to the argument relied on by most of those who contend that machinery can never be injurious to the laboring class, namely, that by cheapening production it creates such an increased demand for the commodity as enables, ere long, a greater number of persons than ever to find employment in producing it. The fact tho too broadly stated is, no doubt, often true.[4]

In more recent times economic writers have offered various opinions. Mr. John A. Hobson, who has discussed the question exhaustively, reaches this conclusion:

> The assumption, however, that machinery must increase the aggregate employment, either in this particular trade itself, or in that trade *plus* the machine making and subsidiary trades, is, of course, unwarranted. All depends upon the effect of the machine in lowering selling price and the effect of the lower selling price upon effective demand. In no two cases will these effects be quite the same.[5]

Professor Pigou, in reviewing the opinions of recent writers, says:

> An occasional failure of this kind is admitted by all. Still, broadly speaking, inventions, as a general rule are believed by those who have studied the matter to increase and not to diminish, employment at the point at which they act. . . . Now I am not concerned to deny the empirical part of these conclusions. I do not dispute the Poor Law Commissioners' assertion that the conditions necessary to

---

3. Babbage, Economy of Machinery and Manufactures, Fourth Edition, 1838, pp. 334–341.
4. J. S. Mill, Principles of Political Economy, 1848, p. 113.
5. J. A. Hobson, The Industrial System, 1909, pp. 280–281.

secure that increased employment in any sphere will ultimately result from an invention in that sphere are, as a matter of practice, usually fulfilled.[6]

Since the question is, as Professor Pigou phrases it, an "empirical" one, a final solution could be reached only by an actual count. It is certain that in some cases no adequate increase in demand occurs. Whether the class of cases in which a fully compensating demand occurs is larger or smaller than that in which it does not, is unknown. Certainly the probability of the occurrence of such a compensating increase in employment is far less than it was thought to be by most of the classical economists.

There is one theoretical consideration which counts heavily against the "usualness" of a compensating increase in production. The saving on direct labor cost for each unit produced, which accompanies the introduction of machinery, is certain, for two reasons, to be in a greater percentage than the reduction in the price of the article. In the first place, the cost of the machinery and royalties must enter into the price. Secondly, the cost of the material is ordinarily not changed by the introduction of machinery. If, therefore, the elasticity of demand for the article is not greater than one, the percentage increase in production will be less than the percentage reduction in the unit labor cost. Under these conditions, unless the rate of wages is reduced by the substitution of cheaper labor, the number of laborers will be reduced.

There is still another consideration applicable to some cases of the introduction of machinery, which makes against the probability of a large increase in demand, occurring within a period of time sufficiently short to benefit the workers already in the trade. Where the use

6. A. C. Pigou, The Economics of Welfare, 1920, pp. 717–718.

of the machine is confined to the patentees or to selected manufactures, the users of the machine may decide that their interests lie in upholding prices rather than in giving the public a larger part of the benefits of the invention. The expansion in demand which might be achieved by lower prices is estimated less highly than the certainty of larger unit profits. Both the Owens Bottle Company and the American Window Glass Company marketed their patents on the principle that less would be gained by a destructive price war, than by taking a considerable part of the market at a more remunerative price.[7] This policy, as has been noted above, operates to retard the introduction of the machine, but it also operates to retard the fall in price.

In the cases of the introduction of machinery studied, the increase in demand within the introductory period, which alone has any effect in bringing about the avoidance of displacement of skill, has been an important factor in one field only, that of the introduction of the linotype. From 1887 to 1895 the cheapening in the cost of composition through the introduction of the linotype did not lead to a compensating increase in demand for labor, but from 1895 on there was a considerable increase in the amount of printing done, which after 1897 was sufficient to compensate for the labor saved by the machine. The character of this increase in demand, however, was peculiar. If it had taken the form of a reduction in price and an increased volume of sales of existing newspapers and magazines, the printers would not have benefited, altho the pressmen would have been helped. Fortunately for the printers, the cheaper cost of composition led to competition among the publishers in the size of the newspapers.[8] Some increase in the

7. The Glass Industry as affected by the War: Tariff Information Series, No. 5, pp. 75, 79, 129.

8. "Introduction of the Linotype," pp. 5, 7.

number of newspapers and magazines and in other kinds of printing was attributable to the cheaper cost of composition, but it was relatively unimportant.

The use of the stone-planer materially lowered the price of cut stone, but the output did not increase. This curious situation was attributed in the trade to the increasing competition of terra-cotta and concrete.[9] After the semi-automatic bottle machine was introduced, the price of wide-mouth bottles — the only kind made at that time on the machine — was reduced somewhat. The increase in production, however, was far from sufficient to compensate for the saving in skilled labor. There was at the time a rapidly widening use of bottles as containers, but the increase in the production of wide-mouth bottles was not appreciably greater than that of other classes of bottles, despite the fact that some users of bottles substituted wide-mouth bottles for narrow-mouth bottles.[1] From 1905 to 1914, the decrease in the price of bottles made on the Owens bottle machine was, as nearly as can be ascertained, about 15 per cent, and the production of all classes of bottles taken together doubled. The rate of increase was no greater in this period, however, for the classes of bottles made on the Owens machine than it had been in the period from 1899 to 1904. The great extension in the use of bottles from 1899 to 1919 appears to have been due primarily to changes in taste which demanded glass-packed goods for sanitary reasons.[2]

In none of the foregoing cases, except that of the linotype, can any considerable degree of increase in production be ascribed with certainty to a reduction in

9. "The Stonecutters' Union and the Stone-Planer," p. 33.

1. "The Introduction of Semi-Automatic Bottle Machinery," pp. 70–71.

2. Ibid., p. 70; "The Introduction of Automatic Bottle Machines," p. 89.

cost due to the introduction of the machine. Other factors, the changes in demand due to taste and the entrance of competing products, played so much the larger part in determining the amount produced during the period of introduction that the effect of price reductions was relatively unimportant.

IV

If the increase in production due to the introduction of machinery were always directly proportional to the displacing power of the machine, displacing power would be only an element in increase in production. Since this is not the case, the displacing power of the machine is to be regarded as a primary factor in determining displacement. A case of high displacing power coming under the observation of Senior was responsible for a modification in the doctrine of a compensating increase in demand. He said:

> A small screw was shown to us at Birmingham which, in the manufacture of corkscrews, performed the work of fifty-nine men; with its assistance one man could cut a spiral groove in as many corkscrew shanks as sixty men could have cut in the same time with the tools previously in use. As the use of corkscrews is limited, it is not probable that the demand for them has sufficiently increased to enable the whole number of laborers previously employed in their manufacture to remain so employed after such an increase in their productive power. Some of the corkscrew makers, therefore, must have been thrown out of work, and the rate of wages in that trade probably fell. . . . The example taken from the manufacture of corkscrews is as unfavorable to the effects of machinery as can be proposed; for the use of the commodity is supposed to be unable to keep up with the increased power of production and the whole number of laborers employed on it is consequently diminished. This, however, is a very rare occurrence. The usual effect of an increase in the facility of producing a commodity is so to increase its consumption as to occasion the employment of more, not less, labor than before.[3]

3. Nassau William Senior, Political Economy, Third Edition, pp. 165–166.

In the cases of the introduction of machinery studied, the displacing power of the machines varied widely. One man on the stone-planer is capable of producing as much as eight men can produce by hand. One man on the semi-automatic bottle machine can make as many bottles as four hand-blowers. A linotype operator can set up as much matter as four hand compositors. The Owens bottle machine in its latest forms is capable of an output per operative equal to that of eighteen hand-blowers. The displacing power of the machine in all the cases studied, as has already been noted, was less at the beginning of the period of introduction, than it was later.

V

The final factor in determining the amount of displacement is the degree to which the skill of the hand-worker is useful in connection with the machine process. This demand for skill may take one or both of two forms. First, the machine may take over only one of several coöperant parts of a trade and leave the other parts of the trade untouched, as in printing, where proof reading and make-up were unaffected by the linotype; or in stonecutting, where carving and some other parts of the work of the stonecutter could not be done by the planer. In such cases, it is possible that a small expansion in demand may be sufficient to retain the same total number of skilled workmen. When, however, the part of the trade affected by the machine is relatively small, the reduction in price is likely also to be small.

This factor was of relatively small importance in salvaging the skill of the stonecutters since, as has been noted above, no increase in demand occurred. The introduction of the linotype, on the contrary, was accompanied by a large increase in the number of proof readers, make-ups and other auxiliary skilled workmen required. This increase was of considerable importance in avoiding displacement, altho, as has been noted above, its full effect was not realized on account of the difficulty of moving compositors on straight matter into other positions.

The second form of the demand for the skill of the handworker in connection with the machine process, occurs where the skill of the handworker is useful in some degree in the working of the machine. Even if there is no increase in the demand for the article, if the skill of the handworker is useful, the employment of part of the handworkers at something more than the wage of an unskilled worker is certain.

The classical economists, for the most part, did not concern themselves with the effects of a change in the quality of the labor caused by the introduction of machinery, since they were intent on the effect of machinery on general wages. They were inclined to minimize the hardships of displacement of skill. Thus McCulloch, after admitting that there may be cases in which there is a reduction in the number of persons employed in the trade affected, says:

> Ultimately, therefore, the introduction of machines cannot fail of being highly advantageous to the laborer; and even when first resorted to, they never impose on him any other hardship than that of occasionally forcing him to change his business. This, however, is seldom a very material one. A person trained to habits of industry and application can be easily moved from one employment to another. . . . It is easy for a weaver of cottons to become a weaver of woolens or linen.[4]

Appropriately enough, Babbage, the discoverer of the fourth principle of the division of labor, was the first writer of distinction to dwell at length upon this aspect

4. McCulloch, Principles of Political Economy, Second Edition, pp. 194–195.

of the problem. After citing statistics as to the increased number of weavers employed after the introduction of power looms, he says:

> In considering this increase of employment, it must be admitted that the two thousand persons thrown out of work are not exactly of the same class as those called into employment by the power-looms. A hand-weaver must possess bodily strength, which is not essential for a person attending a power loom; consequently, women and young persons of both sexes, from fifteen to seventeen years of age, find employment in power-loom factories.[5]

The superiority of the handworker as an operator of the machine over the unskilled worker is a matter of degree. The probability that a machine which performs the work formerly done by skilled handworkers will require for its operation exactly the skill possessed by the handworker must be very small. On the other hand, the probability that the machine will require for its most successful working some part of the skill of the handworker is large. Whether the skill possessed by the handworkers will be salvaged by their employment as operatives depends, therefore, upon several factors: (1) the overhead cost of operating the machine; (2) the degree to which the skill of the handworker contributes to the successful working of the machine; and (3) the relative price of skilled and unskilled labor. The vari-

5. Babbage, Economy of Manufactures, Fourth Edition, p. 339.

A lively appreciation of the effects of the displacement of skill on the handworker led the same writer to offer suggestions as to how the individuals affected might minimize the evil consequences. "Increased intelligence amongst the working classes may enable them to foresee some of those improvements which are likely for a time to affect the value of their labour, and the assistance of Savings Bank and Friendly Societies (the advantages of which can never be too frequently or too strongly pressed upon their attention), may be of some avail in remedying the evil; but it may be useful also to suggest to them, that a diversity of employments amongst the members of one family will tend, in some measure, to mitigate the privations which arise from fluctuation in the value of labour." Ibid., p. 340.

ous combinations of these factors may be illustrated from the history of the introduction of machinery.

When the linotype was being introduced, it was believed by many employers that the machines could be profitably operated by persons who had not had a training as printers. It was soon found, however, that almost every part of the skill of the hand compositor is useful in the working of the machine and that printers were far more efficient than those who had no knowledge of the trade. The overhead cost of the machine — interest, maintenance, rent of space, power, etc. — is almost identical whether the daily output is large or small, and this overhead cost is relatively large in comparison with the daily wage of the operative. Under these conditions a much smaller difference in output between printers and unskilled workers than actually existed would have been sufficient to turn the scale in favor of skilled hand compositors as machine operators.[6]

A somewhat similar situation was presented by the introduction of the semi-automatic bottle machines. Here the skill required was certainly far less than that required for blowing bottles by hand. The issue presented was not, however, whether skilled men should be employed, but whether the bottle-blowers or workmen of a kindred trade — gatherers and pressers — possessed in higher degree the requisite skill. The contest was finally decided, chiefly by the pressure of the blowers' union, in favor of the bottle-blowers. That the bottle-blowers possessed skill which was valuable in the operation of the machines is undoubted. It is equally certain that much of their skill was not useful in the operation of the machine. The output of the machine, however, was directly dependent on the skill of the operators and the overhead cost was large. In a very

6. "The Introduction of the Linotype," pp. 28–29.

short time, the wages paid the machine operators was as high as that of skilled bottle-blowers.[7]

The circumstances attending the introduction of the stone-planer were in some respects favorable to the employment of skilled stonecutters. The output was dependent on the skill of the operative, and some of the skill of the stonecutter was useful in working the planer. The policy of the union in opposing the introduction of the planer, and the relocation of the industry, were largely responsible for the relatively small employment of the stonecutters as planer-men.[8]

The influence of a relatively large wage differential as an obstacle to the employment of handworkers as machine operatives is illustrated by the history of the introduction of automatic bottle machines. When the Owens bottle machine was introduced in 1905, the disparity in wages between bottle-blowers and unskilled workmen was very great. The machine is automatic and its speed is not governed by the attendants. Under these circumstances the attendants were drawn almost entirely from the ranks of unskilled labor. The flow and feed devices for the automatic manufacture of glass bottles, introduced more than a decade after the Owens machines, require somewhat more attention on the part of the attendants than the Owens machine, but their speed also is independent of the attendant. A great change had occurred meanwhile, however, in the relative wages of skilled bottle-blowers and unskilled laborers. While in 1905 a bottle-blower received from three to four times as much as an unskilled laborer, in 1917 unskilled laborers were receiving half as much as bottle-blowers. Altho the amount of skill which the bottle-blowers could contribute to the operation of the

7. "The Introduction of Semi-Automatic Bottle Machinery," p. 83.
8. "The Stonecutters' Union and the Stone-Planer," p. 52.

devices was not large, the employers generally were willing to pay something over and above unskilled wages to secure that skill.[9]

In the cases of the introduction of machinery studied, the five enumerated factors combine in a great variety of ways to bring about great differences in the displacement of skill suffered. The fortunate outcome in the introduction of the linotype was due to the low displacing power of the machine, the large extent of the use of skilled men as coöperant workers and as machine operators, together with an increase in production. The almost equally fortunate outcome in the case of the semi-automatic bottle machine was due to the low displacing power of the machine, the small part of the whole trade involved, the use of skilled men as operators, combined with a rapid increase in the use of almost all forms of glass containers. The great displacement of skill in the introduction of the stone-planer was due to a combination of high displacing power, small use of skilled workers in connection with the machine process, and no expansion in production. A combination of very high displacing power, no use of skilled workers in the machine process, the rapid extension of the machine to the different products of the handworker, despite a very rapid growth in production, was responsible for the disastrous experience of the bottle-blowers with automatic bottle machinery.

The question naturally arises as to whether greater importance may be ascribed to one or more of these factors as against the others. From one point of view the answer is in the negative, since there are doubtless cases of the introduction of machinery in which each of them

9. "The Introduction of Automatic Bottle Machines," pp. 103–104, 113.

assumes a leading rôle. But from another point of view, a line may be drawn between those factors which make for the displacement of skill and those factors which make for its salvage. The strength of the attacking factors — the labor-displacing power of the machine and the rapidity with which it is adapted to the various products and processes of the handworker — is determined by mechanical facts; it may, therefore, be very small or very large. On the other hand, the chief salvaging factors — the increase in demand and the mobility of labor — are economic and work in a medium much less favorable to the attainment of great force. In a group of cases of the introduction of machinery, the variability in the force of the mechanical attacking factors is greater than in that of the economic salvaging factors. From this point of view, therefore, the leading element in determining the displacement of skill is the amount of the disturbance, measured chiefly by the labor-displacing power of the machine and the rapidity with which it invades the trade. If the disturbance is large, the displacement will also, probably, be large.

CHAPTER VI

THE INTRODUCTION OF MACHINERY AND TRADE-UNION POLICY

SUMMARY

In the preceding chapter, in which the factors determining the amount of displacement of skill caused by the introduction of machinery were considered, the discussion was based on the assumption that economic forces were working in a purely competitive régime. The most important modifying influence thus disregarded was the action of the trade unions of the handworkers affected. The present chapter, therefore, is devoted to the various forms of action by which a trade union may lessen or avoid the displacement of skill. The facts have been drawn from the same studies of particular cases that were used in the preceding chapter. In all the cases, at the time of the advent of the machine, there were unions in the trades affected. These trade unions were among the oldest and most powerful in the United States.

The interest of a trade union of handworkers in the introduction of machinery affecting its membership is twofold. In the first place, there is grave danger that the standards of employment of the handworkers may be broken down during the period of introduction. The surplus of skilled men occasioned by the introduction of machinery may be so great as to make it impossible for the union to maintain wages and other conditions of employment at the former level; indeed, the existence of the union may be endangered if the surplus in the trade becomes sufficiently large. Secondly, the union has a sympathetic interest in preventing, as far as may be possible, the reduction of part of its members to the ranks of the unskilled.

These two interests are by no means equal. If a machine threatened within a brief time to displace all the handworkers in the trade, doubtless the interest of the union would lie chiefly in the avoidance of displacement from the trade and not in the maintenance of the standards of the handworkers left in employment. This is rarely, however, the case. Machines are introduced gradually; the scope of the machines is slowly enlarged, until the period of introduction is over. At any given time the union is interested in displacement from the trade chiefly as it reacts upon the working conditions of the skilled men still employed in the trade. It is not, therefore, the avoidance of displacement from the trade which forms the primary concern of the union, but that partial displacement of skill characterized by lower wages and longer hours for the handworkers. Occasionally, as will be illustrated at several points below, these two interests are served by the same policies, but when this is not the case, the union is sure to give preference to those measures which are designed to maintain standards of employment.

Trade-union policies with reference to the introduction of machinery may be divided into five types, according as they are designed: (1) to prevent the introduction of the machine, (2) to increase the amount of work going to the handworkers by decreasing the wage for handwork, (3) to enlarge the field of employment for handworkers so as to include the operation of the machine, (4) to reduce the inflow into the trade, and (5) to distribute more widely the work left to the handworkers. These policies will be considered in order.

(1) Experience has convinced the greater part of well-informed trade-union leaders that the introduction of important labor-saving machinery cannot be permanently halted by trade-union action. In 1905, when the Owens bottle machine was being introduced into the trade, President D. A. Hayes of the Glass Bottle Blowers' Union said, "Working men in England during the first half of the last century fought desperately against the introduction of labor-saving inventions, but always to their own disaster. We have seen many instances of the same kind in this country and the ranks of non-unionism have been augmented thereby."[1] The same opinion has been expressed by many other trade-union officials on numerous occasions and in many reports. Not only is trade unionism officially committed to the view that resistance to machinery is futile, but it is almost unanimous in holding further that resistance to the introduction of machinery delays, or makes impossible, the adoption of measures which may mitigate the hurtful effects of the introduction of machinery.

As a matter of actual practice, however, it not infrequently happens that trade unions do attempt to prevent the introduction of machinery. In the cases of the introduction of machinery examined, such attempts were made by the Flint Glass Workers to stop the introduction of the semi-automatic bottle machine

1. Proceedings, Glass Bottle Blowers, 1905, p. 27.

and by the Stonecutters to stop the introduction of the stone-planer. This divergence between teaching and practice is explained primarily by the simple fact that while the official point of view may be clearly understood, it is not binding on any particular union.

When machinery is first introduced, the line between those displaced from the trade and the survivors has not yet been drawn. Every member of the union is potentially a displaced workman. The only policy, therefore, which fulfills the hope of every member is that of completely stopping the progress of the machine. Where the members feel that the union is very strong in its control of the handworkers or can count on the powerful aid of allied trades, the hopes of the members may prevail against the counsels of their leaders and against the experience voiced by official trade unionism. Particularly is this likely to be the result in those unions in which the formulation of a policy with reference to machinery falls into the hands of the local unions. Where the control of the national union is greater, the likelihood of dealing with the question on a better-informed basis is also greater.

These influences may be illustrated from the histories of the stone-planer and of the semi-automatic glass bottle machine. When the stone-planer was introduced, the national union of the Stonecutters was very weak. In most of the large cities the local unions were entirely independent. The largest of these independent unions — the Chicago union — initiated a campaign against the use of the planer and it spread to the branches of the national union. The policy of opposition thus developed was ultimately forced upon the national union.[2] The forms of opposition varied from place to

2. "The Stonecutters' Union and the Stone-Planer," pp. 35–39.

place and from time to time. In some localities, prohibition of the use of the planer was combined with a rule against the shipment of planer-cut stone from other places. In other unions, a milder form of hindrance in the form of rules restricting the number of planers in proportion to handcutters was in vogue.

The attempt of the Flint Glass Workers' Union to stop the introduction of the semi-automatic bottle machine by requiring the same piece rates on the machine as on handwork is not to be explained by local independence.[3] The Flint Glass Workers' Union is highly centralized and the policy of the union was determined by national officials. These officials did not assent to the general opinion that attempts on the part of a union to prevent the introduction of machinery are likely to be not merely futile, but to retard or prevent the introduction of measures likely to be helpful. The union was very strong and was enforcing at the time many other rules severely restricting production.[4]

Against these attempts to hinder the introduction of machinery, may be placed the frank acceptance of the semi-automatic bottle machine by the Glass Bottle Blowers' Union and of the linotype by the Typographical Union. The same attitude was assumed by the Glass Bottle Blowers' Union when the flow and feed devices for making glass bottles were introduced. The introduction of the Owens bottle machine was peculiar in that the question of union jurisdiction over the machine was not pressed until late in its history, but the Glass Bottle Blowers' Union allowed its members to work at handwork in the plants where the machine was operated by unskilled workers.

3. "The Introduction of Semi-Automatic Bottle Machinery," pp. 73–75.

4. "Regulation and Restriction of Output," Eleventh Special Report of the Commissioner of Labor, Washington, 1904, pp. 624–662.

In both of the instances where the unions opposed the introduction of machines, the results were disastrous. The employers transferred the work to non-union plants or employed non-union men. The unions thus lost the opportunity to use other measures for the avoidance of displacement of skill, which depend for their efficacy upon the extent to which the union controls the industry. That the opposition of these unions did retard the introduction of the machines is undoubted, but no measures were taken looking to the utilization of the period of retardation as a means of salvaging skill. It is not to be inferred from these instances that the policy of opposition is necessarily always unsuccessful. Situations are conceivable in which a union could successfully apply this policy. If the saving by machine production were small, and the control of the union over coöperant workers complete, it is quite possible that a policy of opposition might succeed, at least for a period sufficient to give an opportunity for reducing the number of handworkers. In the cases under consideration, however, the unions failed and in most cases this must be the outcome of such attempts.

(2) From one point of view, the lowering of wage rates may be regarded merely as an attempt to hinder the progress of the machine,[5] but it may more properly be regarded as competition with the machine, involving no more of the element of obstruction than other forms of competition. Sidney and Beatrice Webb in *Industrial Democracy* urged as one of the cardinal points of trade-union policy in dealing with machinery that

5. When the Owens bottle machine was introduced, it was urged by the manufacturers of hand-made glass bottles that if the rates for handwork were reduced at the beginning of the introduction of machinery, the machines would be discarded. The bottle blowers, however, were never willing to accept this opinion. "The Introduction of Automatic Bottle Machines," p. 101.

the rates of the handworkers affected should not be lowered. Their argument in brief runs as follows: The hand product is usually superior at the beginning to the machine-made article. If the handworkers compete in price with the machine, the hand rates must be cut again and again as the machine develops its capacity. The result is that the hand product deteriorates in quality and the market for the hand-made goods grows narrower.[6] In none of the cases of the introduction of machinery studied does this particular argument apply, for in all of these cases, the machine product was quite as salable as the hand product.[7]

The proposal to reduce wage rates on hand composition in order to compete with the machine was made during the introduction of the linotype, but the local unions were strongly advised against the adoption of such a policy. In the opinion of the officials of the national union the reduction required would have been so great as to bring the wages of printers below that of unskilled laborers. A few local unions did pursue this policy, but only for a short time.[8] The stonecutters, for the same reason, did not even seriously consider this method of dealing with the problem presented by the planer.

The only one of the unions which systematically pursued the policy of making reductions on handwork was the bottle blowers, and a review of their experience throws light on the extent to which unions are likely to adopt a similar policy and the consequences likely

6. Webb, "Industrial Democracy," pp. 415, 416.

7. Some newspapers for a time clung to hand composition on the ground of its superiority, but the other advantages of typesetting and type-casting machines over-balanced the advantage of accurate spacing held by hand composition. The machine-made bottle or jar is superior to the hand-made article in exactness of capacity and in finish. Planer-cut stone is not inferior in any particular to hand-cut stone.

8. "The Introduction of the Linotype," pp. 15–16.

to result. The question was first presented to the blowers when the wide-mouth semi-automatic machine for making fruit jars was introduced. The greater part of the production of these jars was in the hands of a few firms, and of these all except one had introduced machines. This particular manufacturer started one of his plants with non-union men. The officials of the union rather than lose control of the other plants, with the full agreement of the workmen concerned, reduced the rates forty-five per cent. The next year the manufacturer introduced machinery.[9]

When the Owens machine was introduced, the officers of the union resisted for several years all proposals to reduce piece rates for handwork, but in 1909 reductions were made. From that time on, the policy of the union was to reduce hand rates on ware made also on the machine, but to maintain rates on bottles which the machine was not capable of making. But this policy was not adopted willingly. It was forced on the union by the threat of the hand manufacturers to break with the union if the concessions were not made.[1] If the manufacture of glass bottles had been sufficiently specialized so that the manufacturers producing ware competing with the machine had been distinct from those producing ware not so competing, the union probably would have refused to grant the reductions. But this was not the case and if the union had refused, it would have lost control not only of the ware competing with the machine product but also very largely of the ware made only by hand.

The experience of the glass bottle blowers in reducing rates to meet the competition of the Owens machine reinforces the opinion that a reduction in the rates for

9. "The Introduction of Semi-Automatic Bottle Machinery," p. 81.
1. "The Introduction of Automatic Bottle Machines," p. 101.

handwork is likely to be ineffective in meeting machine competition. Within a comparatively short period, the ware on which the reductions were made was lost to the hand plants. During the interval, however, more bottle blowers were employed than would have been employed if the reductions had not been made. In the reduction of hand rates on glass bottles, one factor not ordinarily present operated in favor of a larger salvaging of skill than would usually accrue from such reductions. The right to use the Owens machine was granted to only a few manufacturers, each of whom specialized in a special line of ware. These manufacturers centralized their production in large plants. The smaller and more scattered hand plants in some cases had advantages in their proximity to the purchasers of bottles, which partially overcame the lower production costs of the Owens plants. Moreover, the licensees of the Owens Company were reluctant to enter into destructive competition with the hand plants. But even with these advantages, the policy was not successful in salvaging any large amount of skill.

It is not, however, to be assumed that the reduction of rates to meet machine competition is to be condemned under all circumstances. Theoretically, situations may be conceived in which such a policy might be justified, particularly if the only aim of the union were the prevention of displacement from the trade. For example, if the machines were confined to a small part of the work of the trade and the margin between hand and machine cost were small, a policy which combined complete stoppage of inflow into the trade with moderate reductions in prices until the workers in the affected sections could be drawn off into the non-affected sections, might very well result in preventing displacement from the trade.

Practically, however, the difficulty which the union faces is its inability to gain exact knowledge of the facts sufficiently to forecast the trend of events. Moreover, since the union is interested primarily in preserving standards of employment, and since reductions on part of its work are likely to be followed by reductions elsewhere, the policy of lowering wages to compete with the machine is not likely to be adopted except as a measure of preservation.

(3) The policy of demanding the employment of handworkers as machine operators at rates of pay equivalent to those paid handworkers has been urged by some writers as the primary defence of trade unions against the ills which usually follow the introduction of machinery. This policy has three advantages. In the first place, the amount of displacement from the trade will be reduced to the extent that handworkers are employed as operators. Secondly, the danger of a surplus of skilled men is to the same extent avoided. Thirdly, the control of the union is maintained over the entire trade. This policy, therefore, unites in high degree the two aims of the unions — to maintain standards and to lessen displacement from the trade.

The extent to which displacement may thus be avoided is obviously in inverse proportion to the displacing power of the machine. Where the displacing power is low — say one to four — the employment of the handworker as machine operator, particularly if accompanied by some increase in the demand for the article made on the machine, may go far to reduce displacement. These conditions were present in the introduction of the linotype. Where, on the other hand, the displacing power of the machine is high, the requirement that the machine shall be operated by handworkers is not important as a means of avoiding complete displacement, since the number of handworkers who would be absorbed as operators is not large enough materially to affect the result. It would not have lessened the displacement of the bottle blowers very much if skilled blowers had been employed on the Owens machine. The same was true of the stone-planer.

Even, however, where the absorption of handworkers in the machine process is not large, the union may be desirous of securing control over the machine operators, since it will thereby retain control over the entire trade. The union may even secure this control without obtaining any advantages in lessening displacement. Where the union is strong, the employer may be willing to concede union jurisdiction over his machine operators, but may be unwilling to agree to pay a wage high enough to place handworkers on the machine. Under these conditions, control over the machine is secured, but nothing is done toward reducing the amount of displacement.

The chief question with reference to the policy under consideration relates to the extent of its practicability. In some discussions of the subject it is assumed that the enforcement of the rule requiring the employment of handworkers as machine operators at rates equal to those paid for handwork is dependent only on the strength of the union.[2] The great importance and success of this policy in the introduction of the linotype

2. See, for example, the testimony of Mr. Samuel Gompers before the Industrial Commission (Report of the Industrial Commission, vol. VII, p. 615). Mr. Gompers apparently regarded himself as the originator of this policy. In his autobiography, he says: "My office was directly opposite the offices of the International Typographical Union on the same floor. William V. Prescott was then president. It was the time of the introduction of the Mergenthaler typesetting machine in the printing trades. The union had not determined its policy. Again and again, I talked through the problem with Prescott urging him strongly to advocate a policy of not opposing labor-saving machinery, but to plan so that the workman could control the use of the machine through

are well known, and it has been argued that this success was due to the ability of the Typographical Union to force the employment of handworkers as machine operators.[3]

In the previous chapter an analysis was made of the conditions which determine the profitableness of placing handworkers on machines as operators. It was there shown that the outcome in the cases of the introduction of machinery examined corresponded with the incidence of these conditions.[4] An examination of the policies of the unions concerned with reference to the employment of handworkers confirms the conclusion that when these conditions are strongly adverse, they are too potent to be overcome by trade-union action. All the unions were strong unions, but in only one instance — the introduction of the linotype — was the employment of the handworkers secured at wages equal to those formerly received by handworkers. The bottle blowers obtained jurisdiction over the operators of the semi-automatic bottle machine, but only at a lower wage rate than that of handworkers. Some handworkers did take employment on the machines, but

the union instead of permitting the machine to control the printers. The wisdom of the printers in dealing with the issue gave the union a strategic advantage in the development of the printing industry." (S. Gompers, Seventy Years of Life and Labor, p. 373.)

3. Professor John R. Commons in an article in the Outlook of November 1906 (reprinted in Labor and Administration) says, "Perhaps no mechanical invention has worked a greater revolution than the invention of the linotype in the printing trade. It has increased the speed of the operator fivefold. But it made possible a three-months' apprenticeship of girls in place of a three-years' apprenticeship of boys. Yet this substitution did not occur in union offices, because the Typographical Union was able to prevent the introduction of women." (Labor and Administration, p. 127.) The argument in favor of the view that the success of the Typographical Union in securing the exclusive employment of hand compositors as linotype operators was due primarily to the profitableness of using compositors as machine operators is fully set forth in "The Introduction of the Linotype," pp. 28–29.

4. Supra, pp. 134–137.

the number was relatively small. The greater part of the operators were recruited through a special machine apprenticeship.[5] In still another instance, that of the flow and feed device, the union secured employment for its members on the machines, but at wages which were not much above those of unskilled workers. The unprofitableness of employing skilled bottle blowers on the Owens machines was so obvious that the bottle blowers made no attempt to secure their employment.[6]

It may be concluded that the policy of requiring the employment of handworkers as machine operators at wages equal to that of handworkers is one to be carefully explored by a union at the time of the introduction of machinery, but that it is not a policy which is generally practicable. If a large surplus of men in the trade has been caused by the introduction of the machine, the union may wish to secure the employment of handworkers on the machines, even tho the skill of the handworker is not of great value in the operation of the machine, and the rate of remuneration not much higher than that paid for unskilled labor.

(4) The device of directly checking inflow into the trade and thus reducing the amount of displacement during the period of the introduction of machinery can be used effectively by a union only when the national union controls the number of apprentices. This is rarely the case in American trade unions, where this power, when exercised by the union at all, is almost always in the hands of the local unions. In the cases of the introduction of machinery studied, only one of the national unions concerned — The Bottle Blowers — at the time of the introduction of the machine, regulated the number of apprentices by national agreement.

5. "The Introduction of Semi-Automatic Bottle Machinery," p. 80.
6. "The Introduction of Automatic Bottle Machines," pp. 103–104.

Unfortunately for the successful working of this device in the bottle trade, the union and the manufacturers had for many years maintained a system of apprenticeship under which the apprentice was paid much lower piece rates than a journeyman for the same work. The employers were, therefore, reluctant to yield anything in the number of apprentices. Although it was not until comparatively late in the introduction of the Owens machine that the rates received by apprentices were increased, the union was able, by making concessions in wages, to secure reductions in the customary ratio, with the result that the inflow was reduced greatly. Even as it was, many of the apprentices taken from 1908 to 1912 simply increased the number of workmen later forced from the trade. Where it can be used, the direct limitation of the number of apprentices is the most effective device for lessening displacement possessed by trade unions.

In the previous chapter, it was argued that if the mobility of the workers in a trade were sufficiently great — in the absence of any special incentive to the taking of apprentices — the inflow into the trade would cease when there was a surplus of trained men, since employers ordinarily do not profit by training new workers. The promotion of mobility may be regarded, therefore, as an indirect method of checking inflow into the trade. The introduction of machinery is almost always gradual, and a high degree of mobility would make it possible to decrease largely displacement from the trade by the transfer of handworkers (*a*) from the affected branches of the trade to those still unaffected or (*b*) from handwork to machine work, in those cases where the handworkers are employed as operators of the new devices.

The most important attempts at promoting mobility

found in any of the cases of the introduction of machinery studied were those made by the local unions of the Typographical Union at the time of the introduction of the linotype. The national union had established a rule that only journeymen printers could be employed as linotype operators, but it refused to rule that each office must recruit its operators from its own staff of journeymen printers. In the interest of preventing inflow into the trade, it was desirable that operators should be drawn as far as possible from their immediate locality. Otherwise vacancies would have been occasioned in the localities most drawn upon for operators and an inflow of apprentices would have been caused. In order to bring about, as far as possible, local recruitment of operators many of the local unions organized schools for training operators. Also they secured from many employers an agreement that operators should be recruited from the office force. Almost always the local unions granted a reduction in wages during the period of training as a linotype operator.[7]

None of the unions in the trades studied attempted to promote by any organized means, the movement of handworkers from affected branches of the trade to those still unaffected. To have accomplished this would have necessitated either the setting up of some means of retraining the handworker to fit him for another branch of the trade or some concession in wages to employers during a period of training. The first method would have involved a considerable outlay and the second, the possibility of menace to the standard rate.

However desirable mobility from the affected to the unaffected branches of a trade may be as a means of avoiding displacement, the union incurs a risk in promoting it. If the advance of the machine is rapid and

7. "The Introduction of the Linotype," pp. 14–15.

the mobility of the workers in the affected sections of the trade is great, the unaffected sections will soon be over-crowded. A displaced man, who needs aid to make him available, is not a menace to the trade; an army of displaced men made available by training to take the places of men already employed would be a serious problem for the union to face. Since the union is primarily concerned with the maintenance of working conditions, it is not remarkable that efforts in the direction of enhancing mobility have been confined to those required to extend control over the machine process.

(5) The policy of distributing the available work as widely as possible during the period of strain accompanying the introduction of machinery recommends itself to a trade union both as a means of salvaging skill and as a means of lessening pressure on the union's standards. If the number of surplus workmen is not large, a distribution of work may be carried out without materially lowering individual earnings. Whether such a distribution of work is desirable in order to protect standards of employment depends upon whether the displaced handworker is in a position to affect materially by his competition the standards of employment in the trade. Theoretically, therefore, the union would be interested in such a distribution of work chiefly when the displaced men constitute a menace to the maintenance of standards. Practically, it is impossible when machinery is being introduced to foresee how displacement will affect the conditions of employment, and the attempt to effect some distribution of work as a precautionary measure is almost certain to form a part of the union's policy. In the cases studied, the distribution of work was attempted in three ways: (*a*) by rotation in employment, (*b*) by reducing working

time and (*c*) by the introduction of the three-shift system.

(*a*) In some trades, the conditions are such that a full force of workmen is necessary. In a newspaper office, for instance, a certain number of compositors must work if the newspaper is to be published at a fixed hour. Glass bottles when made by hand are manufactured ordinarily by a shop consisting of three workmen, one of whom finishes while the other two blow. If one of the members of the shop is absent, the output is cut in half. Both in newspaper offices and in bottle factories, therefore, it has been customary to employ other workmen to fill the places of compositors and blowers who were absent. In both unions, the choice of a substitute is made by the workman whose position is filled. It was possible, therefore, for the workmen to distribute work during the period of the introduction of machinery.

The printers made much more of this possibility than the bottle blowers. In both unions there was a widespread sentiment that the unemployed should share in the available work, and there was in both unions a considerable amount of voluntary laying-off on the part of the employed in order that the unemployed might share in the work. In the Typographical Union the matter was not left entirely to sentiment, but many of the local printers' unions adopted rules limiting the number of days a "regular" might work in order that "substitutes" might be employed.[8] Among the bottle blowers the matter of "lay-offs" was left entirely to the individual workman regularly employed. The comparatively small interest in this device among the blowers was due to a difference in the character of the invasion of the machine. The introduction of the lino-

8. "The Introduction of the Linotype," p. 18.

type was local in that there always remained in employment in the locality a number of hand compositors. The bottle machines not infrequently completely displaced all the hand blowers in a particular locality. In neither union was the sharing of work a large factor in salvaging skill. It did, however, serve to tide some of the men over a difficult period.

(*b*) A reduction in the hours of the handworkers naturally suggests itself to a union as a remedy for a surplus of workmen. This policy formed a cardinal part of the program of the printers with reference to the introduction of the linotype in newspaper offices. Fortunately, the newspaper publishers were desirous of securing an increase in their ability to set matter in the last few hours before going to press. Under the conditions prevailing before the introduction of the linotype, they were unable to do this except at great expense. With the cheaper cost of machine composition, they did not oppose seriously a shortening of hours for machine operators from those formerly prevailing for hand compositors. Since the office works as a unit, this carried shorter hours for ad-men, proof readers, make-up men and other coöperant handworkers.[9] Neither of the other two unions included in the present study was able to use the device of a shorter work-day as a means of avoiding to some extent the effects of the introduction of machinery. The stonecutters were already working relatively short hours, and technical conditions led the bottle blowers to attempt to reach the same end by means of the three-shift system.

(*c*) At the time the Owens bottle machine was introduced, the bottle hand-plants ordinarily worked two shifts of eight and one-half hours. The employers were strongly opposed to a reduction in the total time worked,

9. "The Introduction of the Linotype," pp. 19–21.

as cost of fuel and other overhead expenses would be increased. To meet this situation, the president of the Glass Bottle Blowers' Union evolved a plan for working three shifts, under which the working time of each shift was to be reduced a full hour. Also, the three-shift system in another way was expected to be an effective means of distributing work more widely. Since a bottle factory while in operation must have men for all its shifts, the existing factories could have absorbed an additional number of workmen equal to fifty per cent of the former force. The factories would not have run as nearly continuously through the year, but the work would have been more evenly divided.[1] The plan was adopted to some extent, but not widely.

The experience of the three unions indicates the difficulties likely to be met in any attempt to distribute work more widely during the period of introduction of machinery. It seems clear that except under very unusual conditions, this device is not likely to be of much effect in reducing the amount of displacement, but as a temporary expedient to relieve the stress of the transition period, it has proved valuable.

The general results of the introduction of machinery in the trades studied may be briefly recapitulated as throwing light on the effect of trade-union action on displacement of skill. The effect of the linotype in displacing workmen from the trade was very small, especially after the early period. The displaced men were chiefly elderly printers who were unable to adapt themselves to either machine work or any of the coöperant processes

1. "The Introduction of Automatic Bottle Machines," pp. 95–97.

required in machine offices. The wages and hours of the handworkers were steadily improved during the period of introduction. Similar results followed the introduction of the semi-automatic bottle machine. The field of invasion here was small relatively to the total trade. A few bottle blowers were displaced, but they were chiefly those who could not accommodate themselves to the other branches of the trade or were unwilling to move to places where work at those branches could be obtained. The conditions of employment were not unfavorably affected; on the contrary, the wages of handworkers were increased and the hours of labor shortened during the period of introduction fully as much as in kindred trades.[2]

The introduction of the stone-planer was accompanied by far less favorable results. Probably one half of the stonecutters in the United States were displaced from the trade between 1900 and 1910. The wages and other working conditions in the trade, however, were only slightly affected. The increase in the wages of stonecutters in this period, one of generally increasing wages, was less than that in some other trades of kindred character, but not materially so.[3] Far more disastrous were the results to the bottle blowers from the introduction of automatic bottle machinery. From 1907 to 1924 the number of blowers and operators of semi-automatic machines decreased from nearly 10,000 to about 1500; in the same period the wages of both these classes of workmen lagged far behind wages in other trades. The bottle blowers advanced their wages very little during this period, while the great mass of American labor more than doubled its wages.[4]

2. "The Introduction of Semi-Automatic Bottle Machinery," p. 82.
3. "The Stonecutters' Union and the Stone-Planer," pp. 59–61.
4. "The Introduction of Automatic Bottle Machines," pp. 104–107, 113–114.

Are these great differences in the amounts of displacement from the trade to any considerable extent explicable on the basis of differences in trade-union policy? It is very doubtful. In the preceding chapter it has been indicated that displacement from these trades agreed roughly with the nature of the mechanical and economic factors which centered around the introduction of the particular machines, and the foregoing study of trade-union policy indicates that these factors are controllable by trade-union action within only very narrow limits.

The effect of differences in trade-union policy on the wages and other conditions of employment of the skilled workers left in employment is a more debatable question. In the foregoing review of the effects of the introduction of machinery, it will have been noted that the stonecutters suffered very little in the matter of wages while the bottle blowers were unable to keep the wages of handworkers on an equality with wages in similar trades. Was this difference due to the policy of the bottle blowers and in particular to their action in reducing the price of articles made on the machine? From one point of view, the answer is in the affirmative. If the bottle blowers had been able to maintain the hand price on articles made both by hand and on the machine, the hand plants would have been forced sooner to abandon the manufacture of those articles. The result would have been an earlier disappearance of the surplus of men in the trade and an earlier upward movement in the wages of hand blowers. This is not, however, to say that the policy of the blowers was inferior to that of the stonecutters. The difference in policy was not due to deliberate choice, but to the difference in the conditions confronting the two unions. The stonecutters are employed by master stonecutters who work on contract, and with a comparatively small investment in equipment. The stonecutters, powerfully aided by the other unions in the building trades, were able to enforce their rates, even in the presence of a large surplus of displaced men. The situation of the bottle blowers was quite different. Their employers had heavy investments in equipment which would have been rendered in large part worthless unless the rates for making bottles was reduced. It was the pressure of these employers, who otherwise would have broken with the union, that forced the blowers to make the reductions.

The most important consideration in determining union policy is the surplus of men in the trade caused by the introduction of machinery and the power of that surplus to affect conditions. A great surplus of stonecutters disappeared rapidly without any markedly injurious effect on working conditions. One of the most striking facts in the history of the introduction of machinery in the glass bottle trade also has been the rapidity with which a surplus of hand blowers became innocuous. It was the rapidly successive introductions of the machine into the various parts of the trade, each of which created a new surplus, that constituted the characteristic difficulty of the bottle blowers in the introduction of the automatic bottle machines.

From the foregoing, two general conclusions may be drawn: (1) The unions have been far more successful in preventing reductions in the wages of the handworkers left in employment by the machine than in lessening displacement from the trade. This is partly due to the fact that the maintenance of working conditions has been the primary aim of the unions, but it is chiefly due to the fact that the amount of displacement from the trade is determined by factors almost entirely beyond the reach of union policy. (2) The policies to be followed by a union during a period of introduction of machinery cannot be stated dogmatically. There are no policies of universal validity. In any particular case of the introduction of machinery, sound policy must be derived from a knowledge of the mechanical and economic factors involved, together with some estimate as to the effect of the surplus occasioned in the trade by the introduction of machinery on the conditions of employment.

Bei Fragen zur Produktsicherheit wenden Sie sich bitte an:
If you have any questions regarding product safety,
please contact:

Walter de Gruyter GmbH
Genthiner Straße 13
10785 Berlin
productsafety@degruyterbrill.com